The US-Japan Security Community

T0386328

Drawing on the work of Karl W. Deutsch, this book argues that the United States and Japan have formed their own security community, based on a sense of "collective identity." In so doing, it provides a new theoretical outlook on co-operation between the United States and Japan, offering a fresh understanding of their bilateral relationship as one that goes beyond a mere military alliance or free trade partnership.

Taking an empirical approach, Sakai analyzes three key case studies: the Persian Gulf War of 1990–1, the terrorist attacks of September 11, 2001, and the Tohoku Earthquake and Tsunami of 2011. He examines how the United States and Japan interacted with one another in their discourses and behaviors in these three instances and thus demonstrates the existence of a collective identity between the two nations.

Hidekazu Sakai is Associate Professor of Kansai Gaidai University, Japan. His research interests include international relations theory, international security, peacebuilding, and Asian-Pacific politics. His recent publications include *Re-rising Japan: Its Strategic Power in International Relations* (2017), co-edited with Yoichiro Sato.

Routledge Studies on the Asia-Pacific Region

For more information about this series, please visit: www.routledge.com/Routledge-Studies-on-the-Asia-Pacific-Region/book-series/RSAPR

The US-Japan Security Community

Theoretical Understanding of Transpacific Relationships

Hidekazu Sakai

Routledge
Taylor & Francis Group

LONDON AND NEW YORK

First published 2019 by Routledge

2 Park Square, Milton Park, Abingdon, Oxfordshire OX14 4RN
52 Vanderbilt Avenue, New York, NY 10017

Routledge is an imprint of the Taylor & Francis Group, an informa business

First issued in paperback 2020

Copyright© 2019 Hidekazu Sakai

British Library Cataloguing-in-Publication Data
A catalogue record for this book is available from the British Library

Library of Congress Cataloging-in-Publication Data
A catalog record has been requested for this book

ISBN: 978-1-138-48667-6 (hbk)
ISBN: 978-0-367-48439-2 (pbk)

Typeset in Times New Roman
by Out of House Publishing

To my wife, Kyoko.

Contents

Acknowledgments

It was impossible to complete this book without inspiration, help, advice, and encouragement from a number of people. The root of this book is my master's thesis, *The New Roles and Characteristics of the United States-Japanese Security Alliance in the Post-Cold War Era*, which I submitted to Department of Political Science of California State University, Fresno in 1993, although its scope is completely different from this book. From time to time during all these years, I presented previous versions of this book's chapters at meetings of Asian Studies on the Pacific Coast (ASPAC) in Honolulu (2007); the International Studies Association (ISA) in New York (2009), New Orleans (2010, 2015), and its international confernce in Hong Kong (2017); the International Convention of Asian Scholars (ICAS) in Adelaide, Australia (2015); and the Asia Pacific Conference of Ritsumeikan Asia-Pacific University (APU) in Beppu, Japan (2015). I am indebted to many comments and much feedback from panel participants and audiences; it is impossible to list all of their names here. Nevertheless, I offer my sincerest gratitude to them for sharpening my thoughts on the security community. Due to limited space, I only can list a handful of people here.

I am grateful to Dr. Russell Mardon, Dr. Marn J. Cha, and Dr. Freemen Wright (deceased), who taught me the foundations of international relations (IR) at California State University, Fresno between 1990 and 1993. I give my appreciation to Dr. Shinobu Yamazaki for his continual friendship since our graduate studies in Fresno in the early 1990s.

I would like to offer special thanks to Dr. Glenn D. Paige (deceased), who taught me nonviolent politics, and its innovative potentiality for IR. His limitless passion for nonkilling global political science took me toward studying the security community. I am grateful to his wife Glenda Paige, who has shared his passion toward a nonkilling global society. I am thankful to Dr. Lou Ann H. Guanson (former Director of the Matsunaga Institute for Peace at the University of Hawaii). I thank Dr. Michael Haas, Dr. Yasumasa Kuroda, Dr. Leslie Sponsel, and Dr. James A. Dator for their magnificent insight on peace studies. I thank Johan Galtung (former Professor of Peace Studies at the University of Hawaii), who taught me the importance of creative thinking on peace. I thank Dr. Ralph Summy for his significant insight on nonviolent political alternatives during his directorship of the Matsunaga Institute for Peace at the University of Hawaii. I thank Mr. Yoshihisa Fujita and Ms. Shizuko Fujita for their untold support and encouragement. I thank Dr. S. P. Udayakumar, Ms. Meera Udyakumar, and Dr. Naruo Yoshikawa for their friendship. I thank Dr. Yukio Tsuda (Professor Emeritus of Tsukuba University), Ms. Mona Ohya, Dr. Minoru Koide (Soka University), Dr. Jay Heffron (Soka University of America), and Mr. Arnold Kawasaki (Soka University of America) for their warm support. I am grateful to Dr. In-Young Kim for unchanged friendship since the days of graduate study at the University of Hawaii at Manoa.

I am sincerely grateful to the Toda Peace Institute (formerly called the Toda Institute for Global Peace and Policy Studies), which granted me a pre-doctoral fellowship (as the first recipient of the Institute) in 1996, and allowed me to participate in its several workshops and conferences elsewhere. I thank Dr. Majida Teheranian (the first Director of the Toda Institute for Peace and former Professor of Communication at the University of Hawaii; deceased). I thank Mr. Tomosaburo Hirano (former Deputy Director of the Toda Institute for Peace; deceased) who taught me the importance of accumulating academic efforts in one's 40s, which will be rewarded in one's 50s. I also thank Dr. Satoko Takahashi (former Deputy Director and Program Manager of the Toda Institute for Peace) for her encouragement. I thank Dr. Olivier Urbain (the second Director of the Toda Institute for Peace), Dr. Kevin Clements (current Director of the Toda Institute for Peace), and Ria Shibata for their friendship.

Special thanks go to my colleagues at Kansai Gaidai University: Dr. Jeff Hester, Dr. Steven Fedorowicsz, Dr. Kazuhiko Nakae, Dr. Tomohiro Uchida, prof. Zoe Jenkins, prof. Peter Edwards, prof. Dawn Booth, and Dr. Maiko Ichihara (currently at Hitotsubashi University), who always cheer me up. I learned many sociological insights on US-Japan relations from Dr. Takeshi Matsuda. I am grateful to Dr. Mark Holstein, with whom I started my doctoral program at the Department of Political Science of the University of Hawaii at Manoa in 1993; amazingly, he has now been my colleague at Kansai Gaidai University for 15 years.

Various scholars influenced my studies, directly or indirectly. I learned magnificent arguments on Japan as the middle power from Dr. Yoshihide Soeya (Keio University). I learned the model of Japan as a peace state from Dr. Stein Tønnesson (Uppsala University). I thank Dr. Yuji Uesugi (Waseda University) for inviting me to various conferences and workshops on conflict resolutions and peacebuilding. I am thankful to Mr. Tony Liu (National Chung Hsing University) and Prof. Tung-Chieh Tsai (National Chung Hsing University) for their invitation to National Chung Hsing Univerity to share my argument on the US-Japan security community with the students.

I am thankful to Dr. Yoichiro Sato (Ritsumeikan Asia-Pacific University), who was an office mate at the Department of Political Science at the University of Hawaii at Manoa in the 1990s when we were PhD candidates, and many years later became my co-editor of *Re-rising Japan* (New York: Peter Lang, 2017). He then 'coincidently' became a series editor of Routledge Studies on the Asia-Pacific Region, the series on which this book is released. I am also grateful to Mr. Simon Bates, Ms. Georgina Bishop, and many others at Routledge for their assistance toward publication.

I am indebted to the following people for the completion of this study: Dr. Kimie Hara (University of Waterloo), Dr. David Welch (University of Waterloo), Dr. Keiko Hirata (California State University, Northridge), Dr. Toshitaka Takeuchi (Osaka University), Dr. Yoneyuki Sugita (Osaka University), Dr. Kyoko Hatakeyama (Kansai Gaidai University), Dr. Philip Streich (Osaka University), Dr. Hiro Katsumata (Tohoku University), Dr. Linus Hagström (Swedish Defense University), Dr. Tadashi Iwami (University of New Zealand), and Dr. William Tow (Australian National University), who gave me invaluable comments on previous drafts of chapters in this book. Special thanks go to Dr. Tsuyoshi Kawasaki (Simon Fraser University) for his elaborate comments and advice on methodology and the logic of my arguments.

Finally, I would like to dedicate this book to my wife Kyoko. She has patiently supported my up-and-down scholastic life since we married. This book is definitely the fruit of our married life.

1 Puzzles

Introduction

A "friend" is someone who behaves altruistically toward another. Altruism is "the belief in or practice of disinterested and selfless concern for the well-being of others" (The New Oxford Dictionary of English, 1998: 50). Friends mutually help and make sacrifices to meet their needs without reward or profit. In international relations (IR), "friend" may have been an excessively naïve and even inappropriate term to be utilized in research. Nevertheless, after the Cold War, IR scholars gradually and consistently have paid attention to friendly international relations (Russet, 1993; Risse-Kappen, 1995; Adler and Barnett, 1998c; Buzan, Wæver, and de Wilde, 1998; Cronin, 1999; Wendt, 1999; Mattern, 2001; Buzan and Hansen, 2009; Kupchan, 2010).

Why have Japan and the United States been friends since 1945? This naïve query grew from my observations, over many years, of postwar US-Japan relations. Japan and the United States fought in the Pacific War that began with Japan's Pearl Harbor attack on December 7, 1941, and ended with the US atomic bombings in Hiroshima on August 6 and in Nagasaki on August 9, 1945. Over generations, American citizens were taught of the military tragedies at Oahu Island, an event which became so synonymous with a contemptible act that the September 11, 2001 terrorist attacks were referred to as "the Second Pearl Harbor." Japanese people have made social efforts to recapture the nuclear attack's tragedies, which instantly killed 120,000 citizens in Hiroshima and 70,000 citizens in Nagasaki and became known as the worst nuclear tragedies ever experienced by humankind. This was symbolized by ICAN (the International Campaign to Abolish Nuclear Weapons), which received the Nobel Peace Prize in 2017. One could believe that these traumatic experiences would hamper the development of a genuine mutual friendship between these two countries. Nevertheless, the Japanese have never considered revenge on the United States for these tragedies. Most Japanese cannot imagine today that there will be another war against the United States, while Americans also no longer consider Japan a military foe.

A similar case is US-German relations. The United States and Germany fought two major wars: World War I and World War II. In World War II, the Bombing of Dresden killed more than 25,000 German citizens. Despite these past tragedies, Germany (once West Germany) has become one of the most trusted US partners in Europe since 1945. A future war between the United States and Germany is unimaginable at present.

US-Japan relations, US-German relations, and an even larger area, the entire North Atlantic (Western Europe, Canada, and the United States) have built the most stable and peaceful relations in the world. Both areas have maintained tight security arrangements and institutionalizations through the North Atlantic Treaty and the US-Japan Security Treaty. Both relationships have shared ideas of liberty, democracy, and the market economy. Nevertheless, while the former area has often been referred to as what IR scholars call a *security community* (Deutsch et al., 1957; Risse-Kappen, 1996; Adler, 1997b, 1998a; Adler and Barnet, 1998c; Ruggie, 1998: 229–39; Adler, 2008), the latter has rarely been considered a case of such a community.[1] This book argues that the US-Japan friendship can be explained as "a security community" by showing their collective identity.

Theoretical Explanations of "Friend" in IR

Conceptualization and discourse on friendship vary among schools of IR. This section will review arguments of the three major schools of friendship: realism, liberalism, and constructivism. In doing so, I will clarify their strengths and weaknesses to explain friendship in IR.

Realism

In the discourse of realism, "friend" is apparently an odd word. As Hobbes (trans. and ed., 1996: 88) stated, "there is always war of everyone against everyone." Realism has been constructed on this premise. Nevertheless, realism is not monolithic. There are as many variants of realism as there are Baskin-Robbins ice cream flavors (Nye and Welch, 2013: 64). Let us survey their arguments on friendship by examining mainly offensive realism, defensive realism, and neo-classical realism, which provide their own sense of friendship.

In realism, a friendship has been translated into an "alliance." The alliance is merely an expedient tool for the state's survival in the anarchical world. The characterization of an alliance is symbolized by the words of Viscount Lord Palmerston: "We have no eternal allies, and we have no perpetual enemies. Our interests are eternal and perpetual, and those interests it is our duty to follow" (Brown, 2003: 82–3). Liska (1962: 12) argues:

> alliances are against, and only derivatively for someone and something ... Cooperation in alliance is in large part the consequence of conflicts with adversaries and may submerge only temporarily the conflicts among allies.

States ally with "the devil" to avoid the hell of military defeat. It is decisively important for the state to ally with the devil (Waltz, 1979: 166). This is far from the sense in which we grasp our intimate relationships with people as friends in our daily life. The suspicious view of other states is presumptuous, and alliance is carefully observed. This reflects the notion that security is scarce in Hobbesian international anarchy, a cognitive tradition that is particularly prominent in the arguments of offensive realism (Rose, 1998: 149; Mearsheimer, 1990).

Defensive realists such as Glaser (1995) tend to be more optimistic about relationships with other states than offensive realists. They tend to view the world as a benign system where security is not scarce, but plentiful. The state often pursues security rather than power, as offensive realists contend. State behavior is usually relaxed and only aggressively responds to external threats (Zakaria, 1998 476–7; Schweller, 1996: 114–15). If there is no geopolitical competition among states, the international system will only be composed of security-seekers. Therefore, status-quo states send signals to revisionist states suggesting procuring defensive weapons as opposed to offensive ones, and they also suggest arms control (Kupchan, 2010: 28–9; Glaser, 1995). For this reason, in contrast with offensive realists, defensive realists stress the importance of communication on intent. This argument can nurture a seed toward something close to friendship if the relationship is not threatened.

Neo-classical realists view the international system as neither Hobbesian nor benign. Rather, they see it as murky and difficult to understand. Neo-classical realists inevitably pay attention to the state-level factor (Rose, 1998: 147, 152–3). This notion leads us to contemplate what state power means for foreign policy making. Zakaria (1998: 9) argues:

Foreign Policy is made not by the nation as a whole but by its government. Consequently, what matters is state power, not national power. State power is that portion of national power the government can extract for its purpose and reflects the ease with which central decision-makers can achieve their ends.

Edelstein (2002) examines how the state invests enormous energy and time to assess intentions of other states for the formulation of foreign policy. Schweller (1998: 21–2) argues that if the state interprets international structure as discontented, it challenges it, even if it is not simply about national survival but about power and prestige. Neoclassical realism insists that the worldview of state leaders plays a major role in international security. Wohlforth (1993) argues the entire history of the Cold War to be a changing cycle of mutual perception between the US and Soviet leaders.

In contrast to Waltz's neorealism and Mearsheimer's offensive realism, defensive realists and neo-classical realists share the notion that each national government's cognitive lens of international structure and other states plays a decisive role for foreign policy. This implies that intergovernmental understanding of foreign policies can reduce uncertainty in the process of foreign policy-making. Transnational policy coordination or policy-making would then alter perceptions between parties and might be a prescription to avoid unnecessary conflicts with other states. This can lead to the concept of a "community of practice," which will be discussed in Chapter 2.

Liberalism

Liberalism stresses cooperation as the central concept in their traditional discourse. Regarding neoliberalism, Keohane (1984) emphasizes the importance of institutions in generating cooperation among states. Cooperation is a mutual adjustment based on active attempts to prevail over disagreements on particular policy areas that arise from common interests. Various economic activities such as trade and monetary, investment, and energy decisions requiring policy coordination are created by international interdependence. This leads to the emergence of an international regime that can sustain itself as an autonomous entity from the hegemonic grips of a particular state (Keohane, 1984: 8–14).

Security organizations are not even an exception. NATO was initially a typical military alliance aimed at assuring Western Europe's security against Soviet threats; its foundation was US unilateral action. Nevertheless, the escalation of the Korean War in the 1950s shocked the United States and European leaders into reevaluating Soviet threats. This led to the "institutionalization" of NATO, which included the integration of West German as well as US forces stationed in European defense positions, with a heavy emphasis on "intra-alliance consultation," with rules, procedures, and processes (Keohane and Wallander, 1999). NATO then transformed into a "security management institution," acquiring various purposes, including partnerships with former Warsaw Pact members and Russia as well as UN military operations.[2] Kawasaki (2007) made a similar argument on the US-Japan security arrangement. It is a case of institutional transformation by adding several layers for regional security, such as the US-Japan-South Korea Trilateral Coordination and Oversight Group (TCOG) for the Korean Peninsula, the Japan–Canada security cooperation, and the ASEAN Regional Forum (ARF).

These institutional liberal arguments on friendship overlap queerly with the realist discourse on alliance. The common characteristic of both arguments on international relations is a "utilitarian" mode (Ruggie, 1998: 23, 28–9); this is the interest-based notion that states are engaged in alignment or cooperation as "a means to an end" for common interests. This type of notion focuses on exogenous factors. Exogenous reasoning is perhaps a minimum impulse toward friendship, but it is still far from altruism-based friendship, unless the discussion steps further toward endogenous factors. To overcome it, Ruggie (1998: 62–84) introduced an ideational element, which he calls "embedded liberalism," that is derived from the discourse of economics. Nevertheless, it cannot promise to generate altruism. Altruism involves self-sacrifice, which is opposed to the presumption of liberal economics that humans are rational actors pursuing the maximization of benefit.

Rather than relying on a discourse of economic and strategic cooperation, Owen (1997: 4–5) emphasizes liberalism as a political ideology. He asserts that only "liberal states" can generate peace with other liberal states. Liberalism contains the seeds of altruism because liberals believe it to be in their interest to respect the rights of others, as long as those others will in turn respect their rights (Owen, 1997: 19). Liberals perceive their circumstances, and the actions that should be taken, through their liberal lens. Liberalism is a worldview that represents an array of individuals and the world (Owen, 1997: 19). The liberal worldview generates "favoritism" on liberal polity among national elites. Their positive identification of themselves as liberals motivates them to seek other liberals with common interests and to create institutions (Owen, 1997: 24–7). This leads national liberal elites to construct good relations with foreign states, having liberal institutions that they objectively judge (Owen,

1997: 49). This argument resonates with the concept of a community of practice, which leads to discussion on the construction of the security community (this will be argued in Chapter 2). Nevertheless, Owen's argument does not inform us of what kind of peace among liberal states emerges as an outcome. Owen's work deepened our understanding of how states "enter" peace by shedding new light on ideational aspects, but does not inform us of what kind of structures or relationships exist among liberal states.

In this regard, Ikenberry (2006: 6, 10) generated his image of the "liberal international structure," which he calls "security co-binding." In it, the United States, Germany, France, the United Kingdom, and Japan are tightly connected in an economic, political, and security partnership. This structure is characterized by the nature of US hegemony, the role of capitalism in solving the issues of relative gains, and a distinctive civic culture (Ikenberry, 2006: 89). The open system of US hegemony has created its empire by invitation (Ikenberry, 2006: 94). He calls an international system based on such a structure the "liberal leviathan" (Ikenberry, 2011).

However, this hegemonic discourse on liberalism excessively stresses hierarchical characters rather than horizontal ones. It is a vertical structure reigned over by the United States. Hence, it is not about mutual exchanges in horizontal relations, and is rather about whether or not the states discussed below accept the US rules discussed above. Echoing Gilpin's (1981) hegemonic stability thesis, Ikenberry's power-oriented notion is incompatible with altruism because altruism does not seek power but rather seeks others' well-being with self-sacrifice.

Constructivism

Constructivists do not view the international anarchical system as a given, as realists or liberalists presume. Rather, they grasp it as transformable, with changes in state identity and their consequent changes in interests (Gould, 1998: 90). Wendt (1992) argues that a "process" of interactions among the states constructs their identities and interests. These arguments overlap with Owen's liberal peace theory, but constructivism's depth is greater. Borrowing many concepts and notions from psychology, constructivists have developed their discourse on how identity can be formed, shared with others, and then become collective. Hogg and Abrams (1988), Stryker (1980), and Cronin (1999: 30) argue that everyone has several conflicting identities that form a "salience hierarchy" that identifies the relative location of one particular identity. The salience hierarchy of identity is dependent upon how much an individual commits to a particular relationship. Likewise, the state maintains its commitment to relationships with other states. The degree of its commitment can determine the salience of identity (Cronin, 1999 31). Mutual recognition among particular states with a high degree of commitment can generate a sense of belonging to a certain group and form the basis for transnational identities (Cronin, 1999 31).

A transnational or collective identity can transform the anarchical character of international relations to a cooperative one (Acharya, 1998: 27; Wendt, 1994). This leads to a discourse on transnational community. Collective identities are not created in an exogenous process, but instead are created and recreated through interaction and socialization (Acharya, 1998: 27). Geographic proximity, given physical location, cultural and linguistic affinities, and a common historical experience are not decisive elements, but processes of interaction and socialization nurture a sense of belonging to a different conception of community from a regional sense, that is, an "imagined community" (Acharya, 1998: 27; Anderson, 2016). Like a nation-state, a security community can be grasped as an "imagined community" (Adler, 1997b: 257–60).

The role of ideology is essentially important for the development of collective identity. Cronin's (1999) studies on "a community of monarchs," "a pan-Italian Community," and "a pan-German Community" suggest the power of ideology, such as the Holy Alliance against nationalism and liberalism, and nationalism tying states together. In particular, Adler (1997b: 257–60) stresses liberal values that can only bring international relations to the most stable and peaceful communities, which Deutsch calls security communities. Liberal values are superior to other value systems such as Nazism or communism because liberal values can make people feel safe and develop mutual trust through civic culture, the role of government, legitimacy, duties of citizenship, and the rule of law. The quality of relationships between people is crucial in such a system. In this sense, Adler agrees with Owen and Ikenberry on the role of liberal values in international friendship.

The Concept of the Security Community

According to Deutsch, who invented the term "security community" in his landmark study with his associates *Political Community and the North Atlantic Area*, published in 1957, a security community is a group of people that has become integrated. Integration means that people within a territory attain a "sense of community," institutions, and practices strong enough and widespread enough to assure dependable peaceful change for a long time. Peaceful change is the resolution of social problems by institutionalized procedures without the use of large-scale physical force (Deutsch et al., 1957: 5). A security community is an entity with real assurance that members of the community will not fight each other physically but will settle disputes in some other way (Deutsch et al., 1957: 5). On the other hand, integration does not necessarily mean the merging of people or governmental units into a single unit.

Deutsch lists two types of security community: the amalgamated security community and the pluralistic security community. An amalgamated security community is the formal merger of two or more previously independent units into a single larger unit with some kind of common government. The United States itself belongs to this category (Deutsch et al., 1957: 6–7). A pluralistic security community, on the other hand, maintains the legal independence of separate national governments. A pluralistic security community is easier to establish and maintain than an amalgamated one (Deutsch, 1978: 244). When we refer to a security community in this study, it will be of the pluralistic type.[3]

Past Studies on Security Communities

Studies on security communities have expanded in subjective and geographical scope since the 1990s. Those studies are on the North Atlantic area, including Austria, Belgium, Denmark, Finland, France, West Germany, Iceland, Ireland, Italy, Luxembourg, the Netherlands, Norway, Portugal, Spain, Sweden, Switzerland, the United Kingdom, Canada, and the United States (Deutsch et al., 1957; Goodby, Buwalda, and Trenin, 2002). Also included in those studies are the North Atlantic Treaty Organization (NATO) (Risse-Kappen, 1996), Western Europe (Wæver, 1998; Bellamy, 2004: 63–87; Kupchan, 2010: 183–283), the Concert of Europe (1815–53) (Kupchan, 2010: 183–283), NATO–Russia relations (Williams and Neumann, 2000), the Organization of Security and Cooperation in Europe (OSCE) (Adler, 1998a), the Euro-Mediterranean area (Attinà, 2000), Northern Europe (Möller, 2003), the Baltic countries (Möller, 2007), the Balkan area (Kavalski, 2008; Moustakis and German, 2009), the Gulf Cooperation Council (GCC) (Barnett and Gause III, 1998; Bellamy, 2004: 118–49; Kupchan, 2010: 183–283), Latin America, North America (Bellamy, 2004: 150–77), US-Mexico relations (Gonzalez and Haggard, 1998), US-Canada relations (Shore, 1998), the Association of Southeast Asian Nations (ASEAN) (Acharya, 1998; Acharya, 2001; Bellamy, 2004: 88–117; Kupchan, 2010: 183–283), ASEAN–US-Australia relations (Chau, 2008), the ASEAN Regional Forum (ARF) (Garofano, 2002), Northeast Asia (Pascha and

Seliger, 2011), South Asia, Southern Africa (Ngoma, 2005), and US-Russia relations (Goodby and Morel, 1993). There are several common inclinations among these works.

First, works of the security community notably tend to look at multilateral organizations, such as NATO, the EU, or ASEAN. However, multiplicity may not matter because the size of a country's geographical space, population, GDP, military, or political power is varied. If we verified the existence of the China–India security community, the combined population would be 2.5 billion, which is roughly one-third of the gross world population. Additionally, US-Canada relations geographically share almost half of a continent.

Second, there is a lack of studies on relations between remote countries separated by vast geographical factors becoming confirmed security communities. There are a handful of case studies on international relations transcending oceans, countries, or continents. When we refer to the term "community," it seems natural to imagine relations with one's neighbors. Nevertheless, it is not necessary to assume that a security community is a neighborhood. Rather, it can be *networks* of countries mutually practising peaceful changes; geography is not destiny (Hemmer and Katzenstein, 2008: 187, 199).

Third, there are insufficient studies on relations between Eastern (Asian) and Western (Western European/United States) countries. A tacit assumption here is that cultural homogeneity derived from common religions, customs, or traditions is a necessary condition for generating mutual trust, shared norms, or collective identity, which are significant factors for the security community. This has led to a relative concentration on Western Europe (or perhaps the whole of Europe) or Southeast Asia. However, Deutsch implies that cultural factors (especially religion) may not be as important as political ideas of democracy or constitutionalism (Deutsch et al., 1957: 124–5).

Finally, there is a peculiar lack of security community studies on US alliances, with the exception of NATO. Since the Cold War began, the United States has built up a worldwide network of alliances, the so-called hub-and-spoke system. Nevertheless, security arrangements such as US-Philippine, US-Taiwanese, US-South Korean, and US-Japanese relationships are not fully examined in terms of security community. These cases understandably assume that maintaining an alliance with the United States is a gate to introducing liberal-democratic norms, pluralistic institutional arrangements,[4] and collective identity. Indeed, the Philippines, Taiwan, South Korea, and Japan are no longer despotic states. They have transformed into democracies today, even though their transformations occurred at different times and under particular conditions. Therefore, it is not peculiar to assume that security communities exist between the United States and its Asian allies.

Why US-Japan Relations?

The case study on US-Japan relations will contribute to security community studies. First, it will advance the understanding of security communities in bilateral relations. The combined gross population of the United States and Japan is more than 400 million; the countries' populations in the world are quite uneven. National leaders and IR scholars (in particular, realists) have considered population as a major source of a state's power and, indeed, major conflicts have occurred among great powers possessing large populations. Hence, bilateral relations deserve attention in addition to regional relations.

Second, the case study can confirm the existence of a security community between remote countries separated by the Pacific Ocean. This would manifest the security community as not only a regionally proximate cohesion but also a *network* of countries transcending geographical factors. This will encourage further research on security communities among various international relations beyond geographical conditions.

Third, the study on the US-Japan case would pave the way for a security study on relations between countries possessing largely different cultural, historical, and ethnic backgrounds. Japan has been influenced by China in all aspects of its lifestyle since ancient times, whereas the United States began its governance as a colony of the British Empire. The major imperial spheres, i.e., the Sino-centrist system or the British Empire, overwhelmingly influenced both countries over centuries regarding their respective state-building, industries, education, food, religion, and lifestyle. Japan and the United States resolutely broke away from these spheres and notably stepped forward to build their own modern sovereign states through the Meiji Restoration and the American Revolution, respectively. However, cultural differences between Japan and the United States still exist.

Fourth, this case study will advance security community studies on US alliances. Japan and the United States began their alliance by signing the US-Japan Security Treaty in 1951 and revised it in 1960; the security alliance is perhaps the oldest one besides NATO (signed in 1949). Both alliances were established as the pivotal components of the US containment policy against the Soviet Union in the early stages of the Cold War.

Finally, we can deepen our understanding of the construction of security communities between countries that fought major wars with each other. This was precisely the case of NATO and Western Europe. Franco-German relations held more than a century-long mutual antagonism through the Franco-Prussian War (1870), World War I, and World War II. Today's Franco-German relations have not only enjoyed a stable peace but have also become the core of Western Europe's security community. A similar argument can also be made for US-British relations from the late nineteenth century onward (Kupchan, 2010: 73–111) or US-German relations in the context of NATO.

Organization of the Book

Chapter 1 discussed the background, puzzles, and research questions that led to the study on the US-Japan security community. This chapter surveyed past studies on the concept of the security community. I noted the tendency for security community studies to concentrate on multilateral organizations and also noted the lack of studies on relations between remote countries separated by geographical factors, relations between Asian and Western nations, and US alliances. This chapter argued that this study can compensate for these "shortcomings." Finally, I indicated the necessity to study the US-Japan collective identity—or the "we-feeling." This chapter stated this book's contribution to the studies on US-Japan relations by showing that the peaceful nature of the relationship can be explained their collective identity, which has led to a confirmation of their security community.

Chapter 2 will describe the theory and methodology. This chapter presents Karl Deutsch's concept of the security community. I will consider the constructivist arguments on the security community from Alexander Wendt, Emanuel Adler and Michael Barnett, and Bruce Cronin as theoretical supplements to Deutsch's concept of the security community. This chapter will then refer to a method to detect the existence of a collective identity. This book will employ Bruce Cronin's "two ways" approach. The first way is to examine the nature of *discourse* between those two countries. The most certain sign is that the United States and Japan have adopted new concepts or vocabularies that would then be publicly articulated. The second way is to analyze *behaviors* of the United States and Japan. It is necessary to determine whether they behave in a manner consistent with their identities in circumstances in which they would otherwise not be expected to do so.

Chapter 3 will test the case of the Persian Gulf War (1990–1). This chapter will reveal how a collective identity emerged from the situation in which the United States demanded Japan's personnel contributions to the war, with Japan struggling to respond. This case involves how the United States reacted to Iraq's invasion of Kuwait by using the United Nations and its international norms, and how Japan made efforts to adhere to them by adjusting its own "norms," based on Article 9 of its constitution. This chapter will reveal the emergence of a collective identity between the United States and Japan through this conflict of norms.

Chapter 4 will examine the terrorist attacks of September 11, 2001 (hereafter "the September 11 attacks"). The September 11 attacks generated another time of trial for the US-Japan alliance. The alliance was not designed to respond to terrorism, and this particular terrorist act did not occur on Japanese soil; thereby, Japan could not exercise its right of self-defense. To assist US forces being deployed in Afghanistan against Osama bin Laden, Japan needed to employ collective self-defense, but a traditional interpretation of Article 9 of its constitution prohibited Japan from using this option. Prime Minister Koizumi seized the initiative with fast legislation enabling JMSDF (Japan Maritime Self-Defense Force) ships to be deployed in the Indian Ocean by bypassing constitutional debates. This chapter will show how the actions of Japan and the United States after the September 11 attacks were different from the case of the Persian Gulf War (1990–1) in their decision-making processes. This chapter will conclude with recognition of their growing collective identity.

Chapter 5 will examine the 2011 Tohoku Earthquake. In particular, this chapter will focus on the US humanitarian assistance and disaster relief, "Operation Tomodachi." This operation mobilized 24,500 US service members, 189 aircrafts, and 24 naval ships of the United States Force, Japan (USFJ). This was the first ever "joint military operation" in US-Japan bilateral alliance history, with the US acting alongside nearly 100,000 servicemen of the Japan Self-Defense Forces (JSDF). This case has a peculiar nature; it was not about war or terrorism, which could visibly reveal "reference others." "Reference others" help actors to form judgments about themselves through comparison and standards of judgment, thus promoting the process of self-definition and, finally, identity formation. As Chapters 3 and 4 argue, Saddham Hussein or Osama bin Laden were reference others because Japan and the United States collectively perceived them as violators of humanity, morality, or the norms of international society. Since I will confirm the collective identity of the United States and Japan without such others, this chapter will recognize their "strong" collective identity.

Chapter 6 will argue that the state of the US-Japan relationship is judged as a security community. Collective identity appears as "altruism" in relations between the United States and Japan. This is consistent with what Adler and Barnett call "the mature stage" beyond the "nascent" and "ascendant stages" of the security community's evolutionary path. This chapter will present my findings drawn from the case studies conducted herein.

Notes

1 There are a handful of works on this subject. Taku Ishikawa, "Alliances in Security Communities: Theoretical Perspectives on Compatibility," in *An Alliance for Engagement: Building Cooperation in Security Relations with China,* edited by Benjamin L. Self and Jeffery W. Thompson (Washington, DC: The Henry L. Stimson Center, 2002), 30–53; Hidekazu Sakai, "Anzen Hoshō Kyōdōtai to Shite no Nichibei Kankei," *Hōsei Rongyō* 41(1) (November 2004): 270–82. Nevertheless, these works failed to confirm the existence of a transnational collective identity between Japan and the United States.
2 Neorealist Waltz agrees with this argument. See Kenneth N. Waltz, "Structural Realism after the Cold War," *International Security* 25(1) (summer 2000): 20.
3 Deutsch and his colleagues recognized the following 13 relations as pluralistic security communities: United States–Canada since around 1819, United States–Britain since 1871, United States–Mexico since the 1930s, Norway–Sweden since 1907, Sweden–Denmark and Denmark–Norway since the late nineteenth or early twentieth century, Austria–Germany between 1876 and 1932, Britain–the Netherlands, Britain–Belgium, and Belgium–the Netherlands since 1928 (if not earlier), Britain–Norway, Britain–Denmark, and Britain–Sweden since 1910 or earlier. See Deutsch, Karl W. et al. (1957).
4 Steve Weber argues that the initial American behavior in the postwar period toward constructing a security arrangement with Britain, France, and West Germany, which later evolved into NATO, was based on a multilateral principle that was the reflection of the American tradition of political pluralism. See Steve Weber, "Shaping the Postwar Balance of Power: Multilateralism in NATO," in *Multilateralism Matters: The Theory and Praxis of an Institutional Form,* edited by John Gerald Ruggie (New York: Columbia University Press, 1993), 233–92.

2   Theory and Methodology

Introduction

Deutsch views the construction of a security community as a product of a dynamic process through the flow of exchanges and transactions in personal, material, and ideal levels that cross national boundaries. Such communications are likely to nurture mutual sympathy and loyalties of "we-feeling," trust, and mutual consideration. Deutsch insists that trust-building and a new identity based on the sense of community are decisively important features because peaceful change cannot be assured without them (Deutsch et al., 1957: 36).

Deutsch pays great attention to the flow of communication as the cause of a new identity. Political elites and decision-makers redirect their attention and behaviors through communication with their prospective partners in the process of community-building. Deutsch's definition of communication is:

> The ability to give these messages from other political units adequate weight in the making of their own decisions, to perceive the needs of the populations and elites of these other units, and to respond to them quickly and adequately in terms of political or economic action.
>
> (Deutsch et al., 1957: 40)

Deutsch aimed to describe the process by which former enemy states develop amicability toward each other in transnational interactions and rarely resort to war. Such communications cement sociopolitical groups that cross national boundaries; they are most likely to produce the mechanism for peaceful changes or dispute settlements. Institutionalized procedures for smooth transactions are increasingly embedded in the societies of each country. This eliminates the possibility of war among member states of a community (Deutsch et al., 1957: 5).

The Security Community as a Social Construction

Deutsch and his associates (1957) chose the quantitative approach to study the transaction flows among nation-states to confirm the existence of a security community. They gauged how frequently personal-material-institutional exchanges occur with technological advancements in transportation and communication. Nevertheless, Deutsch's excessive emphasis on quantitative measures overlooked social relations that were derived from and expanded by the transactions (Kegley and Wittkopf, 1984: 187; Haas, 1973: 117; Morse, 1972; Adler and Barnett, 1998a: 9). Deutsch failed to determine what kind of social relations emerge from transnational interactions, how they evolve, what institutions are generated, and what values are shared. For these reasons, Deutsch's theory was long neglected, and studies of transnational transactions largely focused on concepts of international interdependence and, later, the international regimes of the liberalists (Adler and Barnett, 1998a: 9).

Nearly four decades later, Adler and Barnett (1998c) aimed to overcome these shortcomings by fusing Deutsch's concepts with constructivism. They understand the security community as a social construction. They consider constructivism a suitable theoretical framework to provide qualitative views on how societies change and evolve thorough mutual communications that cross national boundaries.[1]

Adler and Barnett (1998b) describe a community as follows. The members of a community enjoy shared identities, values, and meanings. They are involved in face-to-face encounters in various ways. Community members exhibit a reciprocity that indicates long-term common interests and even altruism (Adler and Barnett, 1998b: 31). Community can be created through a high degree of reciprocity that demonstrates how members' interests are interchangeable. Although members of a community may still compete with each other, they no longer fear the use of violence as a means to resolve their conflicts (Adler and Barnett, 1998b: 32).

Technological advancements in the modern era have enabled people to facilitate a sense of community among those who are not physically present together (Cohen, 1987: 298). It is possible to imagine a community of states in geographically remote areas. The sense of community is not dependent upon geographical proximity but on the way identities, values, and meanings are shared (Adler and Barnett, 1998b: 32–3). This phenomenon led me to imagine the existence of a security community between the United States and Japan that is separated by the Pacific Ocean.

Deutsch (1957) argues that the prominent difference between the security community and other kinds of community is whether there are "dependable expectations of peaceful change." States must possess war-avoidance practices to join the community of democratic states in the contemporary era (Adler and Barnett, 1998b: 34). Although Adler and Barnett (1998b) are fully in agreement with this premise, they pay attention to "how" dependable expectations of peaceful change can be confirmed. Peaceful change is the absence of preparation for organized violence as a means to settle interstate disputes. This means that states not only do not undertake but also do not "consider" actions that can be interpreted by others within the community as militarily threatening. Therefore, security communities come to exist when there are tacit and/or formal normative prohibitions for member states to settle their disputes through military means (Adler and Barnett, 1998b: 35). Deutsch (1957) expects some sort of cohesion among a population that is generated not only by self-enforcement mechanisms from below, but also by enforcement from above.

Nevertheless, a community would not be a security community if it relied on enforcement. Some collective norms are not only regulative but also designed to solve collective action problems in relation to inter-dependent options and constitutive and direct reflections of the state's identity and self-understanding (Adler and Barnett, 1998b: 35–6). This means that security community governance relies on an understanding of member states' behavior at the international level as well as an interpretation of their domestic behavior and arrangements. Whereas Deutsch (1957) focused on external aspects of interstate practices and transnational forces, Adler and Barnett (1998b: 36) argue the need to consider "domestic" behavior in ways that are consistent with the community.

Process is vitally important. Process involves transactions, inter-national organization and institution, and social learning. Institutions and organizations can directly promote mutual trust and shared iden-tity. They facilitate and encourage transactions and trust by establishing norms of actions, monitoring mechanisms, and sanctions to impose those norms. This was a hallmark of Deutsch's (1957) theoretical framework. Nevertheless, Adler and Barnett (1998c) go beyond this in suggesting that institutions "encourage member states to discover their preferences, re-conceptualize who they are, and re-imagine their social bonds.

Social learning is a key factor. Communication among political elites generates a process of the redefinition and reinterpretation of reality—"what people consider real, possible and desirable—on the basis of new causal normative knowledge" (Adler, 1991: 52, 1997a: 339). Therefore, social learning is not just an adaptation or response by political leaders to the new reality or environment through pragmatic means. It is a transformation of the beliefs and identity of political leaders, social leaders, or agents that may even lead to an alteration of the realities they face. Social learning can occur on a mass level, but policy-makers and political, economic, and intellectual elites are the most crucial social segments in forming a security community (Adler and Barnett, 1998b, 44–5). This forms "a community of practice," as will be discussed later in this chapter.

According to Alder and Barnett, the ideal status of a security community is that member states have mutual trust and collective identity that are necessary for the development of a dependable expectation of peaceful change. Trust and identity are reciprocal and reinforcing. The development of trust can strengthen mutual identification. Once some measures of trust develop, a collective identity is likely to be strengthened and increases the depth of trust. This is directly related to my argument about the "evolutionary path of collective identity" later in this chapter.

In this situation, there is no need to monitor member states' trust through institutional–organizational arrangements. Instead, knowledge and belief play the major roles. Judgment based on years of experiences and encounters generates the cultural definition of a threat. Identity begins with the understanding of oneself in relation to others. In other words, identity is defined socially by the actor's interaction with others and in relation to others (Adler and Barnett, 1998b: 45–8). The probability of war between member states becomes extremely low. It is unimaginable for them to think of preparing for armed conflicts against each other.

Conditions for the Existence of a Security Community

Deutsch argues that a pluralistic security community requires three essential conditions for its existence: the compatibility of major values, mutual response, and the mutual predictability of behaviors (Deutsch, 1957: 66–9).[2] The compatibility of major values can be translated into *norms*; mutual response can be conceptualized as *institutions*; and the mutual predictability of behaviors can be understood as *collective identity*.[3]

The first condition is norms. Deutsch argues that the values of political ideology that constitute constitutionalism, democracy, and mixed economy are significantly important, whereas religions seem less important (Deutsch, 1957: 124–5). The domestic liberal–conservative division seems less significant as long as liberals and conservatives both genuinely adhere to the framework of constitutional democracy with a mixed economy and operate within it (Deutsch, 1957: 27, 124–5).[4] This involves the way member states share their norms in terms of each body politic.

Norms are a central part of any social community. Norms are standards of behavior that are defined in terms of obligations and rights. Norms shape actors' senses of normal and abnormal behavior, coordinate expectations and reduce uncertainty, influence decision-making, and justify actions and the actions of others (Acharya, 2001: 24; Kratochwil, 1989: 59). Norms are not only a regulative concept but also a constitutive one. Although norms can prescribe and regulate behavior, they also define and constitute actors' identities. Norms can generate not only expectations about how actors will behave, but also learning opportunities (Acharya, 2001: 24; Checkel, 1998: 345). More importantly, norms are entities independent from the power relations or material conditions that endorse them. Norms can impact state behavior, shape state interests, and generate collective interests and identities (Acharya, 2001: 24).

The second condition is institutions, or the capacity of the participating political units or governments to respond quickly and adequately to each other's needs, messages, and actions, without resorting to violence. This is a matter of mutual sympathy and loyalties. It involves a "we-feeling," trust, and consideration of identification regarding self-images and interests; the ability to predict each other's behavior; and the ability to act in accordance with that prediction (Deutsch, 1957: 129). It is a dynamic process (i.e., social learning). This requires constant communication. Peaceful change cannot be assured without a continuous learning process, together with a continuous process of keeping in touch to prevent unlearning (Deutsch, 1957: 130). This inevitably requires arrangements for communication on a regular basis. Thus, institutional arrangements are required among partners in the form of treaties, declarations, regular consultations through summit meetings, ministerial meetings or vice-ministerial meetings, joint committees, domestic legal arrangements, and special treatments.

Institutions affect and transform state interests and behaviors. Institutions not only regulate state behaviors but can also constitute state identity. State interests and behaviors are not innate; they are products of the processes of interaction and socialization (Acharya, 2001: 22). Institutions can shape state practices by establishing, articulating, and transmitting norms that define what constitutes acceptable and legitimate state behavior. In other words, institutions can be a site of interests and identity formation (Adler, 1997a: 345).

The third condition is the mutual predictability of behavior (Deutsch et al., 1957: 56–58, 1978: 244–5). This can be translated into collective identity. The member states of a pluralistic community must make joint decisions on limited policy areas. At the same time, the member states maintain their independent decision-making power within national boundaries (Deutsch et al., 1957: 67). It would not be possible to enter into such a decision without a "sense of we-feeling" or collective identity because such decisions demand that the member states prepare for self-sacrifices, financial contributions, or diplomatic risks.

Identity is directly related to the "we-feeling" that Deutsch recognized as the most important feature of a security community. Deutsch views the development of security communities as an exercise in identity-building, defined as some degree of generalized common identity or loyalty (Acharya, 2001: 27). In constructivism, collective identities are created and recreated through interactions and socialization, just as norms are contested and created and recreated through politics (Acharya, 2001: 27). Collective identity can transcend geographical proximity, cultural and linguistic differences, and historical experiences. "Imagined communities" can be made through processes of interaction and socialization among member states (Acharya, 2001: 27).

The Community of Practice

The key to affirming the existence of the collective identity of a democratic coalition is whether there is "a community of practice" that involves a transnational circle of political elites and decision-makers. This community of practice constitutes like-minded groups of practitioners who are informally as well as contextually bounded by a shared interest in learning and applying a common practice (Adler, 2008: 199). The existence of such a group is important because no country in the world can expect smooth, peaceful interstate relations unless both nations possesses a collective identity. This is reinforced by power struggles within a country. In both Japan and the United States, there is an internal diffusion of powers—such as the administrative branch (interbureau or intrabureau relations), the legislature (ruling–opposition or majority–minority relations), or factions within parties or the cabinet. One difficulty in governing in a democracy is that any national government has to address such scattered powers and somehow seek consensus. The policy generated by consensus may irritate or displease intimate foreign states because of unexpected policy outcomes. However, if a community of practice exists, it can expand gradually at the political-social level. Policy outcomes can then change in the way the intimate foreign state prefers in the long term (Adler, 2008: 196–7).

In an unprecedented role, some of the cabinet members, politicians, and bureaucrats in Japan have generated a new identity through the policy-making process. An emerging community of practice promoted a new identity within American–Japanese circles of political leaders and governmental officials, including US Congress members, Japanese Diet members, the president and prime minister, officials of the US Department of State, the US Department of Defense, the White House, the Japanese Cabinet Office, the Japanese Ministry of Foreign Affairs, the Japanese Ministry of Finance, and the Defense Agency (later, the Japanese Ministry of Defense). The transnational circle initiated the materialization of unprecedented security policies and expanded its size within political elites to change identities.

Making a Hypothesis on the US-Japan Collective Identity

Among these three conditions, this study focuses on collective identity. The reasons are as follows. In the case of NATO, there were already democratic states, i.e., the United Kingdom and France. A collective identity as liberal democracies was an incentive for the United Kingdom and the United States to organize their alliance. Their views of threats were not merely based on military concerns, but were also about postwar economic instability and the risk of the collapse of the domestic order of Western Europe, which would induce communism (Risse-Kappen, 1996: 361, 373–8). Hence, their identity as liberal democracies played a major role in Western Europe's collective actions since that time. Identity was a largely independent variable, whereas institutions (NATO or the EU) and norms (values of democratic polity, free trade, and human rights) were both independent and dependent variables.

In contrast, the US-Japan alliance was not an outcome of Japan's democratization. It was a pragmatic arrangement for Japan's postwar survival. The first priority of the Japanese Government, headed by Prime Minister Shigeru Yoshida, during the US occupation of Japan (1945–52) was to recover its national sovereignty. However, Japan did not possess enough armed forces for its national defense because the United States had destroyed all of the Japanese armed forces in accordance with the 1945 Potsdam Declaration. Yoshida considered an armed force a minimum requirement for national independence. Yoshida's initial idea was to defend Japan with the United Nations' police forces, but he soon realized that this was an unrealistic goal. Yoshida then elaborated his idea that Japan would keep US forces stationed in Japan for a "trade-off" with the restoration of Japan's independence from the United States, because this perfectly matched US desires to contain the Soviet Union in Asia (Hara, 1992: 16–23; Muroyama, 1992a: 45–61). Establishing a US-Japanese alliance was about the restoration of the minimal conditions of the state's existence, rather than an ideological commitment to democracy. Indeed, Yoshida was doubtful that Japan would transform into a democracy (Dower, 2000: 65, 84, 225–6). Yoshida himself was *not* a democrat but a royalist, anti-militarist, and anti-communist (Hara, 2005: 62–5, 112, 129, 133, 223–35). Yoshida firmly opposed Japan's alignment with Nazi Germany and Fascist Italy in the 1930s and favored cooperation with the United Kingdom and the United States simply because it would secure Japan's survival in the balance of power in world politics, rather than an ideological commitment to democracy (Hara, 2005: 79–85).

Although norms and institutions can be generated in a relatively short term, the emergence of a new identity requires a long time, especially with a new collective identity (Adler and Barnett, 1998b: 50–8). Therefore, norms and institutions are independent variables, whereas collective identity is a dependent variable when examining postwar US-Japan relations.

Japan became a "democracy" after World War II. After Japan's surrender in 1945, the SCAP (Supreme Commander for the Allied Powers), which was composed substantially of US forces, occupied Japan for seven years. The SCAP, led by General Douglas MacArthur, carried out radical reforms, such as transplanting liberal democracy by making a new constitution, disbanding all armed forces, implementing state–church separation, humanizing Emperor Hirohito, promoting equal rights for men and women, denying belligerent education, implementing agrarian reforms, and promoting freedom of the press, all of which MacArthur considered necessary measures to eliminate feudalistic elements from Japanese society.

Japan transformed its own identity to accommodate this series of radical normative and institutional changes in the short period immediately after World War II. Yoshikazu Sakamoto argues that Japanese laborers, students, and intellectuals, on both the right and the left, identified themselves as democrats by 1947 when the SCAP changed its orientation of occupational policies due to the beginning of the Cold War. The SCAP's implementation of the "red purge" after 1947 caused stormy debates at the social level regarding whether Japan was truly a democracy when it expelled communists or leftists while rightists or militarists rehabilitated their status. The SCAP's democratic reform was already indigenized and then evolved into mass movements in 1951. Shigeru Nanbara, the president of the University of Tokyo, made a speech in the United States in 1949 stating that Japan should arrange a peace treaty with all belligerent nations of World War II, including the Soviet Union. This speech inspired the Japanese people to protest in the name of the "defense of democracy" (*minshushugi yōgo*), ironically against SCAP's anti-communist stance because the mass movement's basic position was that there was no democracy if particular political groups or ideologies were excluded (Sakamoto, 1987: 64–6).

This situation deserves attention with regard to Japan's identity changes. Japan's democratization did not yield its collective identity with the United States instantly. Japan's democratic identity was tolerant to socialism, whereas the United States drew a rigid line between democracy and socialism-communism. The Japan Socialist Party (JSP) remained a significant political power until 1993. Nanbara's insistence on an overall peace treaty in the 1940s and students' protests against the revision of the US-Japan Security Treaty in the 1950s exemplify strong leftism and even anti-US sympathies in Japanese society. Furthermore, many crimes associated with the issue of US military bases in Okinawa hampered the generation of a collective identity with the United States. Many Japanese saw the US military deployment as the extension of US occupation.

With these arguments, I arrived at an inquiry regarding whether Japan has generated a *collective identity* with the United States. Past studies on this issue are not supportive. Risse-Kappen (1996: 398) believes that the US-Japan alliance has failed to generate a collective identity at the same level as NATO, although it has developed institutional arrangements throughout the Cold War era. Berger (1996: 317–56, 1998: 135–6) argues that Japan has maintained a norm of antimilitarism beyond the Cold War, which was initially planted by the US occupational forces in the immediate postwar era. Ironically, this hampered the formation of Japan's collective identity with the United States in the post-Cold War era. Samuels (2007: 14) argues that postwar democratic Japan received a cheap ride with the alliance with the United States. The core of the Japanese identity is maintained by keeping a distance from Western civilization and not being overwhelmed by Western culture (Samuels, 2007 201; Kitaoka, 2000).

Pyle (2007: 13, 33–7, 45–8) made a similar but broader argument based on his deep historical observations of Japan's own civilization. Japan was able to maintain its own civilization and culture thanks to its geographical isolation from the empires of China. Japan successfully avoided becoming a tributary state to China until the nineteenth century; this was training for Japan in the modern era when the predatory imperial powers of Europe colonized its Asian neighbors. Japan's relationship with the United States after World War II is a similar case. Japan's behavior in the international system has been highly pragmatic, and has not been driven by the great transcendent ideals or universal principles that the United States has strongly maintained (Pyle, 2007: 45–6, 48). The US-Japan alliance is a pragmatic entity without sharing an ideological affinity. Pyle stresses Japan's high flexibility and adaptability to the existing international order based upon certain norms. This was the case of the present international liberal order led by the United States as well as the Sino-centric order in premodern periods. Following Pyle's argument, Japan would not develop its shared or collective identity with any country while adopting governing or dominant international norms.

In contrast, Katzenstein presents his subtle views on the US-Japan collective identity. He argues that in their identification with Europe in the 1940s, US officials typically mentioned religious-democratic values and race as the foundation of a North Atlantic community, whereas these are absent in the case of Asia (Hemmer and Katzenstein, 2008: 197). Nevertheless, the United States treated Japan and the Philippines in slightly different manners from Southeast Asian countries because the United States, Japan, and the Philippines shared historical experiences (the war and subsequent occupation of Japan and the colonization of the Philippines) that could provide some basis for identification. Identification is not a matter of all-or-nothing, but of degree (Hemmer and Katzenstein, 2008: 205–6). If Katzenstein is correct, it is possible to assume the existence of collective identity in the long term while the United States and Japan have shared norms and institutions.

Citing Hegel, Cronin argues for the relative consciousness of individuals in social contexts. One's ethnicity only becomes apparent when one comes into contact with other ethnic groups; ethnicity is not a defining characteristic in a uni-ethnic group (Cronin, 1999: 25; Hegel, 1967: 38, 320).[5] In this regard, the West (democratic free trade countries), including Japan, can be understood as a uni-ethnic group. Japan can be exemplified as a black-eyed population within a uni-ethnic group (the West) that is conscious about eye color as socially significant. Once this ethnic group (the West) encounters a different ethnic group (the Non-West: communists, dictators, Islamic fundamentalists), eye color is no longer an important characteristic.

In this sense, although many have observed that Japan and the United States are "different," the nature of recognition was *not* identical with the nature of recognizing the Soviet Union. Japan transformed into a liberal democracy after 1945 and entered the alliance with the United States in 1951. Japan joined the United Nations in 1956 and has since maintained its diplomatic principle of tight relationships with liberal democracies (MOFA, 1957). Japan is an original member of the Group of Six (with France, the United Kingdom, West Germany, Italy, and the United States), which has led to regular summit meetings since the first in France in 1975 and has evolved into a political fortress against the Soviet Union's worldwide expansionism.

Changes in Self/Others

The study of identity in international relations includes at least two elements. The first is state identity, the concept that the self and the other are unique. The second element is transnational identity—the self–other conceptions that include broader social categories shared by at least two states (transnational identity) (Cronin, 1999: 23–4). This relationship is complex. Parochial state identities emerge from the state's understanding of itself as different in many ways from other states. Although domestic politics and national cultures play a significant role in promoting state identity, they are influenced by the state's participation in international society (Cronin, 1999: 24; Mead, 1934). Human identity is not innate. Identity cannot exist without relationships with others because if the individual were completely autonomous from society, there would be no need to identify itself (Cronin, 1999: 24). In other words, an identity is created through contact with others.

According to symbolic interactionist theories, actors hold multiple "selves" with each related to the interactions with which he or she is involved (Cronin, 1999: 25; Mead, 1934). Each actor, therefore, is a unique combination of various characteristics and social locations. As we interact with others, we become conscious of ourselves as objects (as well as subjects) and come to recognize, assess, judge, and create identity.

The significance of an individual's identity for understanding behavior is often dependent upon the particular social situation. Actors often know what to expect of each other in particular situations because they know that many kinds of people behave in typical ways in particular situations (Cronin, 1999: 25; Hewitt 1976). In this regard, it is necessary to examine a particular situation—such as a war, crisis, depression, or terrorism in which Japan behaved as a part of a security community or not. Thus, identities are "situated" within specific contexts. Once the self appears, it continues to be defined and re-defined through interactions (Cronin, 1999: 25).

An emergency provides an opportunity to confirm collective identity because it reveals to what extent an assisting country is devoted to its sacrifice. This manifests as rapidity of response, budget size, numbers of involved persons, quality of scope, amendments to laws and legislation, and national support of assisting countries. These provide clues to confirm the importance of a suffering country to an assisting country. This could be an international interest as an extension of national interests, a large scale of self-sacrifices, and prevailing altruism.

As we shift from one situated identity to another, we develop an accumulated sense of the others who are important to us, either positively or negatively. Sociologists refer to these as "reference others" or "reference groups" (Cronin, 1999: 25; Shibutani, 1955). Reference others help actors to form judgments about themselves by comparing judgment standards and thus promoting the process of self-definition and finally identity formation. Actors continually compare themselves to others, positively or negatively, in part to better define who they are and, equally importantly, who they are not (Cronin, 1999: 25).

Furthermore, others do *not* have to be other states; they can be the country's own past. This may involve self-reflexive differentiation practices that treat a past condition of the state as the reference point. This was the case of the European Union when it opened up the possibility of the construction of a political identity through a less-exclusive practice of temporal difference (Rumelili, 2007: 27).

For these reasons, this study tests three cases of national emergency: the Persian Gulf War during 1990–1, the September 11 terrorist attacks in 2001, and the Tohoku Earthquake in 2011. These case studies will reveal whether the United States and Japan have a collective identity. Japan and the United States identify themselves as liberal democracies that value international law and humanity. Hence, this study assumes as others: Saddam Hussein (Chapter 3), who invaded Kuwait, thus violating the sovereignty of a neighboring country; and Osama bin Laden (Chapter 4), who plotted terrorism against the American people. I see Japan's rejection of the US disaster relief mission for the 1995 Great Hanshin Earthquake in the past (Chapter 5) as "others" in the collaborative operations of US forces in Japan (USFJ) and the Japanese Self-Defense Forces (JSDF) for the 2011 Tohoku Earthquake.

Detecting Collective Identity

How can we detect the existence of a collective identity? Cronin proposes two paths. The first is to examine the nature of *discourse* among specific political actors. Discourses conducted in terms of collective identity are clear acknowledgments of a group's existence. They constitute a recognition that the actor wishes to be identified with the group (Cronin, 1999: 15). The most certain sign that a group has adopted a new concept or understanding is *the development of a new vocabulary* that is publicly articulated (Cronin, 1999: 15). Specifically, we need to judge whether a group characterizes others with whom it interacts, both positively and negatively, or whether the group speaks of a special bond among specified actors (Cronin, 1999: 15). It is possible to hypothesize that the United States and Japan identified each other as like-minded, liberal-democratic states.

The second way is to analyze the *behaviors* of the actors. We need to determine whether the specified actors behave in a manner consistent with their identities in circumstances in which they would otherwise not be expected to do so. Several elements serve as evidence of collective identity through behavior. First, we must ascertain whether specific actors from different states *act as partners, rather than adversaries or competitors*, in their deliberations and interactions. Second, we need to ensure the existence of *a clear concept of a group interest or common good* among member states. Third, we must confirm whether the actors share *collective strategic perspectives*. Finally, if we recognize that these perspectives *influenced the process and outcome of the deliberations*, they will count as evidence for the constitutive power of identity (Cronin, 1999: 16–17).

Conclusion

This chapter presented the theory of the security community and argued that a security community is a social construction. Deutsch advocates that member states within a security community have a dependable expectation of peaceful change. Adler and Barnett advanced this claim by theorizing how this occurs through three developmental stages: nascent, ascendant, and mature.

This chapter then presented three conditions for the existence of the security community: norms, institutions, and collective identity. Whereas norms and institutions can be shared in a relatively short time, the emergence of collective identity requires a longer term. In particular, the case of the United States and Japan illustrates this emergence. In contrast to Western Europe, Japan was not a democracy when the United States occupied it after World War II. The Western bloc was formed from its strong commitment to liberal democracy against the communist Eastern bloc, but the US-Japan alliance began from a pragmatic motivation for Japan's physical survival rather than an ideological commitment to democracy. This study presumes that the formation of this collective identity began in the post-Cold War era. Since Soviet threats no longer exist, the genuine identity of a democracy, not simply an anti-communist identity, can be tested by comparing "others" such as dictators and terrorists.

This chapter then presented the methodology to confirm a collective identity. It examined the nature of discourse and the behaviors of the states. In so doing, it is possible to measure whether US-Japan relations have moved in a direction of positive identity and ultimately toward symbiosis.

Finally, this chapter suggested an evolutionary path of collective identity. This path can be divided into the three stages—of emergence, growth, and cementing. At the stage of emergence, a community of practice exercises leadership to achieve transnationally common policy goals despite strong domestic oppositions. If a community of practice pursues something beyond parochial national interest, it can be judged as the emergence of collective identity. At the stage of growth, a community of practice develops, and national consciousness about a partner country at the mass level grows. This reinforces the development of collective identity. The strong existence of collective identity is confirmed at the stage of cementing. Collective identity now becomes an independent variable to control the development of norms and institutionalization.

Notes

1 Wendt also argued that Deutsch was a forerunner of "constructivists." See Alexander Wendt, "Collective Identity Formation and the International State," *American Political Science Review* 88(2) (June 1994): 384.
2 Deutsch lists 12 conditions for an "amalgamated security community (namely the United States itself)" and stresses three conditions for "pluralistic security community (security community comprising of the independent sovereign states)." See Deutsch et al. (1957: 66–9).
3 Acharya examined these three conditions to confirm the existence of a security community in Southeast Asia. See Amitav Acharya, *Constructing a Security Community in Southeast Asia: ASEAN and the Problem of Regional Order* (London: Routledge, 2001).

4 It must be noted that Deutsch is less confident about value compatibility in economy because the scale of governmental intervention and control are varied among European-North American countries. Nevertheless, he says that these differences would not hamper pluralistic integration among them. See Deutsch et al. (1957: 124–5, 27).

5 Also see translator's note 320 in G. W. F. Hegel, *Philosophy of Right*, translated by T. M. Knox (New York: Oxford University Press, 1967), 38, section 40.

3 Emerging Collective Identity
The Persian Gulf War (1990–1)

Introduction

This chapter will examine the discourse and behaviors taking place between the United States and Japan from August 2, 1990, when Iraq militarily invaded Kuwait, to April 26, 1991, when the Japan Self-Defense Force's (JSDF) minesweepers left for the Persian Gulf. In so doing, we will analyze how Japan and the United States interacted with each other in light of Iraq's invasion and whether they identified themselves differently from Iraq.

There are several reasons why I chose the case of the Persian Gulf War (1990–1). The first concerns timing. The Persian Gulf War was the first major armed conflict following the Cold War. If Japan and the United States had nurtured their collective identity by this time, this critical situation would have provided evidence of it. There should have been a cumulative sense of important "others," either positively or negatively. Assuming a generated collective identity while recognizing a shared "reference others," i.e., the Soviet Union during the Cold War, the collective identity or "we-feeling" could also be found in the context of the Persian Gulf War. In this conflict, Saddam Hussein was viewed as the new "reference others" as he was a dictator violating international law by invading a neighbor. However, Japan was arguably only a democratic ally of the United States in East Asia following the Cold War era. Hence, the Persian Gulf War is a good case for confirming the US-Japan collective identity. If we can confirm it, the state of US-Japanese relations can be judged as being at the "mature" stage of a security community, as referred to by Adler and Barnet.[1]

Second, there is the significance of the Persian Gulf War's geographic factor. The Persian Gulf War occurred outside of East Asia, where the US-Japan security alliance was presumed to respond. It is natural that Japan would not readily cooperate with the United States. Furthermore,

Japan never provided combat aid to US wars outside East Asia after 1945. Although Japan imports most of its oil from the Middle East, this factor would not necessarily lead to military-related activities by the JSDF to secure it, despite the fact that this might limit logistical support to US combat operations. Thus, if Japan had cooperated with the United States in war, it would have demonstrated the existence of the "we-feeling" of the US-Japan relationship, overcoming geographic factors.

Third, the war was a serious challenge to the pacifist norm in postwar Japan. The United States sought Japanese military cooperation despite the strictly defensive posture of the JSDF, which was based on Article 9 of the Japanese Constitution. This was not the first time. In the late 1960s, US President Lyndon Johnson asked Japanese Prime Minister Eisaku Sato for permission to use the US Air Force base in Okinawa to bomb North Vietnam, which Sato granted. In the case of the Gulf War, Japan not only accepted US use of Okinawa bases for the war but also attempted to send its own sailors and airmen into the conflict zone. The reactive difference of Japan between the two wars may hint at the significant change of interest by the Japanese with respect to cooperating with the United States over time. As Yamaguchi (1992) notes, Japan gradually responded to US demands for security cooperation over the entire course of postwar history. Among these demands, the Gulf War represented a prominent extension of such behavior by Japan. Therefore, the Persian Gulf War (1990–1) is a good case for understanding how Japanese national interests became "international interests" regarding the removal of Iraqi forces from Kuwait through the process of identity change for the United States and Japan. According to Wendt, national interest is not given but can be changed as state identity changes (Wendt, 1992, 1994).

Finally, the Persian Gulf War is a difficult case (Eckstein, 1975). Waltz (1979: 125) argues, "If we observe outcomes that the theory leads us to expect, even though strong forces work against them, the theory will begin to command belief." The war is often referred to as a grim case in that the United States did not appreciate Japan's enormous financial and military cooperation. Americans saw the Japanese as "paying money, not blood or sweat." On the other hand, the Japanese saw such American attitudes as "belligerent" and "high-handed" (Kato, 1995: 215–16).

Puzzle

There are some puzzles in the Persian Gulf War. The United States asked Japan not only for financial assistance but also for manpower, i.e., the dispatch of the JSDF to the Persian Gulf region. While the former request was granted, the latter was refused. Manpower aid was constitutionally and politically infeasible for Japan before the outbreak of the war in January. Nevertheless, Japan undertook enormous efforts to grant the request despite the high political risk it would incur by challenging its postwar constitutional ban on sending Japanese troops overseas. Japanese Prime Minister Toshiki Kaifu, a strong "dove" politician, recognized such a risk. Japan's challenge in sending civilian aircraft and cargo ships, a medical team, the United Nations Peace Cooperation (UNPC), bill JSDF aircraft, and minesweepers was connected to the enormous difficulties presented by a number of political and constitutional concerns. Katzenstein (1996) and Berger (1996) describe these difficulties as the norm of anti-militarism. However, despite this norm, and even after the end of the war, Japan still sought to dispatch the JSDF to the Persian Gulf, although the United States no longer required assistance.

Such behavior by Japan was in sharp contrast to that of China, Asia's sole Asian permanent member on the UN Security Council. Unlike Japan, China did not support military intervention, did not commit troops to the multinational coalition, and did not make a financial contribution (Calabrese, 1993: 479). China initially supported UN Resolution 678 on the withdrawal of Iraqi forces from Kuwait, but it refused to participate in the military coalition by abstaining from the final vote (Harris, 1991: 118; Calabrese, 1993: 478). Rather, China supported peaceful resolution within the Arab world rather than Western military intervention (Shichor, 1992: 93). China suspected the military interference in the region as representing a US interest in dominating oil production there. US military intervention in the Gulf region violated China's "non-interference" policy, which was a component of the Five Principles needed for normal international relations.[2] This behavior on the part of China was also a tacit protest against the existing Western-centric world order (Huo, 1992: 269–70).

How do we understand Japan's behaviors? Existing studies may provide some insights. Calder (1988) characterizes Japan as a "reactive state." He argues that Japan cannot take major policy initiatives in international affairs because of its domestically fragmented structure regarding political decision-making, such as bureaucratic sectionalism or factionalism in the ruling Liberal Democratic Party (LDP). The only way to implement major policy changes in Japan is through external pressure (*gaiatsu*) from a foreign country, particularly the United States (Calder, 1988). From this view, Japan's financial contribution to the war can be understood as an outcome of successful US *gaiatsu* (external pressure). Nevertheless, it cannot explain why the United States failed to secure Japanese military-related aid during the war. Kuroda (2001: 111–12) suggests the strong pacifism prevalent among the Japanese public as a possible "intervening variable." However, this variable still cannot account for Japan's *own* continual effort to send JMSDF minesweepers in the post-Persian Gulf War period, given the dramatically decreasing pressure by the US following the end of the war and the remaining strong domestic pacifism after the war.

Richard Samuels explains Japan's JSDF dispatch efforts during the war as a "normalization" process for Japan. Normalization denotes that Japan behaves consistently according to the preamble of Japan's constitution and the UN Charter on collective security. Samuels (2007: 65–7) argues that the Secretary-General of the LDP, Ichiro Ozawa, aimed to achieve JSDF participation in the multinational coalition as a part of the process. This was Japan's first attempt to become a "normal state." Ozawa was the most powerful figure in the LDP. He was also a strong proponent of Japan's participations in international security activities (Ozawa, 1993). Nevertheless, it was a question of whether Ozawa's motive was genuinely derived from such an international commitment rather than a caring bilateral partnership with the United States.[3]

"The role identity" account provides some insight. According to Catalinac's discourse analysis on the Japanese Diet members' statements from August 1, 1990 to April 30, 1991, the "pacifist" identity was more salient in Japan than the "pragmatic multilateralist" and "centrist" identities (Catalinac, 2007).[4] She argues that the strong pacifist identity may be a major factor behind Japan's failure to send the JSDF to the Gulf region during the war (Catalinac, 2007: 90–1). However, this explanation cannot explain why the Kaifu Cabinet intended to respond to US requests despite the prevalent pacifism in the Diet. Her conclusion was drawn solely from policy outcomes rather than policy-making. Nevertheless, we need to examine the nature of the Japanese Government's politically risky efforts to carry out the SDF overseas dispatch during that time.

There is also the puzzling behavior of the United States. First, US requests for physical support were limited to logistical support or non-combat activities, such as the removal of underwater mines, loading weaponry by roll-on/roll-off ships, or air transportation of war refugees. The United States used its various channels to make these happen. Such aid was merely "minor support" and was not decisively important for the United States to carry out the war. The United States was undoubtedly the sole military superpower after the Cold War. Why did it want physical support from Japan? Second, the United States was aware of Japan's constitutional constraints preventing it from deploying its armed forces beyond its national boundaries. Following the war, US Ambassador to Japan Michael Armacost confessed that he had no desire to see Japan dispatch combat troops overseas (Armacost, 1996: 101). Why did the United States want Japan to send the JSDF from so far away?

Snyder's (1997) alliance management account may explain these actions by the US.

Snyder argues that there is "alliance dependence" between allies. Allies will be more dependent on each other's support as threats from their enemy appear. Countries rely on their allies more heavily when threats from an adversary become greater (Snyder, 1997: 30–1). Applying this account to the Persian Gulf War, we can develop the following explanation. After the Cold War ended, US military power declined in absolute terms; therefore, the United States was not powerful enough to fight against Iraq alone. The United States was now "dependent" on Japan and thus needed the JSDF. Conversely, the United States bargained over this issue with Japan by using Japan's "dependence" on US military protection of Japan.

The former explanation, however, is weak because the problem could have been solved easily by acquiring military support from the North Atlantic Treaty Organization (NATO). NATO is geographically more accessible to the Persian Gulf than Japan and is more powerful than the JSDF. The United States urgently needed aircraft and ships that could transport US forces deployed in Europe to Saudi Arabia immediately following the onset of the Persian Gulf crisis (GRIPS, 2005: 39). Hence, it is natural that NATO would carry out the mission. Furthermore, the US-Japan security alliance was designed to function exclusively in East Asia. Therefore, it is highly unlikely that the United States would have requested Japan to be a part of a war operation in the Middle East. The latter account is also unpersuasive either because US military deployment in Japan is *not* only for Japan but also for its own national security interests, or because its bases in Japan, particularly Okinawa, had been the cornerstone of US forward deployment around the world. The United States used the Okinawa bases to mobilize US forces for the Persian Gulf War.

In short, none of arguments above can effectively account for the behaviors of Japan and the United States. Rather, we could arrive at a comprehensive explanation of both countries' actions by two-way thinking on identity between the United States and Japan. Collective identity generates collective interests that formulate particular policies. Therefore, this article hypothesizes that there was a "collective identity" shared by the United States and Japan in the war.

The Persian Gulf War (1990–1991)

Discourse

Let us scrutinize the discourse conducted between the United States and Japan. The United States took the initiative in forming an anti-Saddam multinational coalition immediately after Iraq's invasion of Kuwait in August 1990. The United States actively cooperated with the Soviet Union, NATO, and Arab states. Therefore, the nature of the discourse on collective identity must be grasped as something concerning the United States not only by itself but also as part of a multinational coalition.

Iraq invaded Kuwait on August 2, 1990. Soviet President Mikhail Gorbachev described the first US-Soviet attempt at joint crisis management as "a kind of solidarity that has never been expressed before in the history of the world" (Dobbs, 1990). The Soviet Union even referred to the possibility of it joining in multinational military action (Remnick, 1990). After returning to Washington, US President George Bush addressed Congress, stating:

> I just returned from a very productive meeting with Soviet President Gorbachev. And I am pleased that we are working together to build a new relationship. In Helsinki, our joint statement affirmed to the world our shared resolve to counter Iraq's threat to peace. Let me quote: "we are united in the belief that Iraq's aggression must not be tolerated. No peaceful international order is possible if larger states can devour their smaller neighbors." Clearly, no longer can a dictator count on East-West confrontation to stymie concerted United Nations action against aggression. A new partnership of nations has begun.
>
> We stand today at a unique and extraordinary moment. The crisis in the Persian Gulf, as grave as it is, also offers a rare opportunity to move toward an historic period of cooperation. Out of these troubled times, our fifth objective—a new world order—can emerge; a new era—freer from the threat of terror, stronger in the pursuit of justice, and more secure in the quest for peace. An era in which the nations of the world, East and West, North and South, can prosper and live in harmony. A hundred generations have searched for this elusive path to peace, while a thousand wars raged across the span of human endeavor. Today that new world is struggling to be born, a world quite different from the one we've known. A world where the rule of law supplants the rule of jungle. A world in which

nations recognize the shared responsibility for freedom and justice. A world where the strong respect the rights of the weak. This is the vision that I shared with President Gorbachev in Helsinki. He and other leaders from Europe, the Gulf, and around the world understand that how we manage this crisis today could shape the future for generations to come.

(Bush, 1990)

Gorbachev stressed that US-Soviet collaborative actions in November were a requirement to produce a UN resolution for military options against Iraq. He said, "we cannot let Saddam Hussein and his regime bring the international community to its knees." Gorbachev added that there had been a "common decision" to discuss the possible use of military force (Devroy, 1990). Although the Soviet Union later decided not to join collective military action, Soviet leadership showed its close alignment throughout the crisis and its subsequent war the following year.

NATO showed unanimous support for the United States against Iraq. None of the NATO member states expressed any reservations about confronting a threat unrelated to the Soviet Union or the Warsaw Pact (Drozdiak, 1990a). British Prime Minister Margaret Thatcher said in August that the allies cannot "expect the US to go on bearing major military and defense burdens worldwide, acting in effect as the world's policeman" (Drozdiak, 1990b). Italian Foreign Minister Gianni de Michelis remarked that Western European states should "dig into [their] purses to assist nations such as Turkey, Jordan, Egypt that are suffering from the global ban on trade with Iraq" (Drozdiak, 1990b). However, West German Defense Minister Gerhard Stoltenberg made clear that West German troops would not be sent to the Gulf region because of constitutional limitations (Fisher, 1990a). However, less than 48 hours later, he stated that West Germany would dispatch its minesweepers and other warships to the Mediterranean Sea, which was a part of NATO defense zone, having overcome constitutional constraints (Fisher, 1990b).

The United States then reaffirmed its long alliance with Saudi Arabia to secure fuel for US military operations (Wines, 1990). Baker sought cooperation from Yemen, which had been on close terms with Iraq (Hoffman, 1990). The first contingent of several thousand Egyptian troops arrived in northeastern Saudi Arabia, which was 80 miles west of the Kuwait border (Claiborne, 1990a). Syrian troops were then sent to Saudi Arabia to join Egyptian forces (Claiborne, 1990b). Baker announced coordination with Syria on "collective efforts" to isolate

Iraq a week after the Iraqi invasion. The United States approached Iran, which had been an enemy of Iraq.

As others, Saddam's Iraq was a violator of international law. Bush repeatedly referred to Saddam Hussein as "Hitler" during the crisis. The US-led multinational coalition identified itself as a legitimate force with UN authorization, thus contrasting itself to Iraq's position as a squatter in Kuwait. To generate a sense of otherness regarding Iraq, the United States invoked the Nazi or Fascist aggression of the 1930s. When the UN Security Council unanimously declared on August 9, 1990, that Iraq's annexation of Kuwait was "null and void," US Ambassador to the United Nations Thomas Pickering said:

> There is something repugnant, chilling, and vaguely familiar about the statement issued yesterday by the Iraqi Revolutionary Council. We have heard that rhetoric before. It was used about the Rhineland, the Sudetenland, about the Polish Corridor, about Mussolini's invasion of Ethiopia and the Marco Polo Bridge incident in China ... The world community did not react. The result was global conflagration. We here will not and cannot let this happen again.
>
> (Goshko, 1990)

While the United States was forming a multinational coalition, Japan took prompt action against the Iraqi invasion. On August 5, one day prior to the passage of the UN resolution against Iraq, Kaifu officially demanded that Iraq withdraw from Kuwait by threatening economic sanctions, including the freezing of Iraqi assets and a trade embargo (*Asahi Shimbun*, 1990, August 6, Evening Edition: 1, 2). Japan froze Kuwait's assets in Japan entirely so that Iraq would not be able to use them (Iokibe and Miyagi, 2013: 24–6). Bush commented on this action as follows: "I pay respect to the Japanese government's prompt and effective measure. In terms of Japan's important role, this measure will send a good signal to the whole world" (*Asahi Shimbun*, 1990, August 6, Evening Edition: 2).

Nevertheless, a discrepancy in their discourse soon emerged. Bush made a telephone call to Kaifu on August 14 (Japan time) (*Asahi Shimbun*, 1990, August 14, Evening Edition: 1). During the conversation, Bush asserted that Japan must send its "minesweepers" to the Persian Gulf, even while the Soviet Union was considering dispatching its navy to the region. Kaifu resisted Bush on the grounds of Japan's constitutional constraints (*Asahi Shimbun*, 1990, October 16, 1990: 1; Kunimasa, 1999: 22–3; Teshima, 1993: 112–13). Bush also asked for Kaifu's commitment to "common interests." This tells us that their interests were not entirely compatible. The term "common interests," as used the by the United States was simply not only to condemn what Iraq did to Kuwait but also to expel Iraq's forces from the country. This required physical means. Japan began considering what it could do for such purposes other than financial aid. Kaifu delivered a speech at New York University in September 28, stating, "The United States should not shoulder responsibility on maintenance of the world order alone any more. The countries that share the basic values must share their responsibilities" (*Asahi Shimbun*, 1990, September 29, Evening Edition: 1). At the US-Japan summit meeting on August 29, Bush told Kaifu that if the JSDFs contributed to transportation, logistics, and medicine without resorting to force, it would be welcomed (Kunimasa, 1999: 61–2; Teshima, 1993: 154).

The United States expected Japan to become a visible part of the US-led multinational coalition, while Japan comprehended the Gulf crisis merely through the lens of the United Nations rather than the United States. When Japan referred to the multinational coalition, it was as a UN-authorized force *rather than* a US commanding force. Kaifu's initial eagerness to create "the United Nations Cooperation Corps (UNCC)" in October symbolized this view. The UNCC comprised unarmed civilian units in addition to the existing JSDF. Kaifu's initial image of the unit resembled the American Peace Corps.[5] After the US-Japan summit meeting in September, Kaifu urged the passage of the UNPC bill that inaugurated the UNCC with its 1,000 members providing non-combat aid, such as communication support, surveillance, truck repairs, and medical support to the US-led multinational coalition force.

The Japanese Ministry of Foreign Affairs (MOFA) insisted that the UNCC must be a civilian unit entirely independent of the JSDF. According to MOFA, SDF officers must resign to the JSDF first and then join the UNCC The Japan Defense Agency (JDA) flatly refused this idea. It was unthinkable for the JDA that former JSDF officers would operate military ships, airplanes, or equipment out of the JSDF chain of command (*Asahi Shimbun*, 1990, November 29: 2; Kunimasa, 1999: 105, 108–12).

Similar battles occurred within the ruling LDP. Kaifu stated, "I will make JSDF officers take off their uniforms, join UNCC and send them." A major factional leader of the LDP, Michio Watanabe, replied, "If you do that, they just become manual laborers. Although we will send drivers or pilots, there will be no vehicles or airplanes. I don't care if they wear red or blue uniforms. But there is no point unless we use them all together" (Kunimasa, 1999: 107). Similar battles occurred elsewhere within the executive branch of the LDP (Kuinimasa, 1999: 107–8, 115–16). After the stormy debate, the LDP finally submitted the UNPC bill to the Diet on October 16. Nevertheless, the bill was rejected by the Diet on November 10.

The United States intentionally distanced itself from this domestic turmoil. Armacost avoided giving any advice on the Japanese Government and the LDP. He was aware that the bill was highly sensitive to the Japanese in general and that any remarks by him would complicate US-Japan relations.[6] On the evening of January 16 (US time), US State Secretary James Baker informed the Japanese Ambassador to the United States, Ryohei Murata, that the multinational coalition would be entering the war momentarily. Baker continued, "Considering the very tensed atmosphere in America, we need your active contributions. We sincerely need the Japanese government's immediate and definite decisions" (Murata, 2008: 115).[7]

In summary, the United States and Japan spoke of themselves as a part of the multinational anti-Saddam coalition. The vocabulary used or developed as mentioned above indicated that both Japan and the United States were part of a group that would not permit Iraq's violation of international norms, even though there was a slight difference in their way of expressing this view.

The term "new world order" in Bush's speech at the US Congress in September 1990 symbolizes firm determination by the United States to intervene in the crisis in a collective sense. With the multinational coalition, the United States used other words, such as "solidarity," "international community," "common decision," "common interests," and "collective efforts." Furthermore, Bush repeatedly referred to Saddam as a violator of international laws. The US-led multinational coalition identified itself as a legitimate force with UN authorization—in contrast to Iraq, which was identified as a squatter in Kuwait (Freund, 1990: C1). Bush described Saddam as "an aggressive dictator threatening his neighbors" and compared him to Adolf Hitler. He continued, "As it has so many times before, it may take time and tremendous effort, but most of all, it will take unity of purpose. As I have witnessed throughout my life in both war and peace, America has never wavered when her purpose is driven by principle" (Apple, 1990). This "otherness" was shared by Japan, as seen in Kaifu's statements.

The United States often used the terms "responsibility" or "vision." These words conveyed US consciousness of its leadership in shaping a "new world order." This would denote that the military option was inevitably to be shouldered by the United States. On the other hand, Japan frequently used the word "contribution (kōken)" during the entire crisis.

"Contribution" did not specify whom Japan would provide aid to or for what purposes it would be used. Indeed, Japan's decision on an additional $9 billion financial "contribution" in January 1991 left a loose end as to whether Japanese money would be allocated exclusively to the United States or shared with other members of the multinational coalition (Armacost, 1996: 122; Iokibe and Miyagi, 2013: 40–1).

There was even negativity in their discourse. A high-profile example was the US congressional reaction to Japan's financial aid of $3 billion announced in September 1990 (Blustein, 1990: A1). US lawmakers saw this as "too little, too late" (Ishihara, 1997: 69; Murata, 2008: 111). Senator Lloyd Bentsen (Democrat, Texas) stated, "Japan has done little [in the Gulf] to uphold its interest and even that has been done quite grudgingly." Senator John Heinz (Republican, Pennsylvania) said that Japan needed to formulate "a clear idea of what their responsibility was to the rest of the Free World." Senator Frank Murkowski (Republican, Alaska) said that Japan has no soldiers at risk in the region. The US and other Western allies "put up the maximum resources, namely human resources, and Japan is excluded" (Burgess and Reid, 1990, October 6, 1990: A24). This was a reflection of US dissatisfaction with what Japan would truly offer in the anti-Saddam fight. However, we can interpret these words as showing considerable frustration derived from the US's high expectations of Japan as an ally in the first place. Indeed, this expectation continued until the last moment before the outbreak of a war as Baker spoke of "active contributions" and "immediate and definite decisions" in conversations with Murata.

Behaviors

The United States consistently requested Japan's *physical and military* aid from the beginning of the crisis in August 1990 to the brink of war in January 1991. Kaifu was coincidently scheduled to visit five countries in the Gulf region—Turkey, Saudi Arabia, Oman, Jordan, and Egypt—from August 15 to 27, as previously planned (*Asahi Shimbun*, 1990, August 7: 2). The United States was supportive on this tour because it was perfect timing for Japan to extend forthright political support to Gulf countries facing severe domestic and foreign pressure caused by the crisis (Armacost, 1996: 101–2). That said, Kaifu decided to cancel the trip because Japan could appear greedy, as if attempting to squeeze oil out of them (Reid, 1990a, August 14, 1990: A16).

Kaifu's decision led the United States to pressure Japan to dispatch "Japanese manpower" to the region (Armacost, 1996: 102). As already seen in the discourse section, Bush asked Kaifu to send the JSDF minesweepers to the Gulf region. US requests for physical aid then went back and forth between Washington and Tokyo. In Washington, Ambassador Murata met a number of US officials in August, including State Deputy Secretary Lawrence Eagleburger, State Undersecretary Robert Kimmitt, Principal Deputy Assistant Secretary of State for East Asia and Pacific Desaix Anderson, Special Assistant to the President Karl Jackson, Chief of Japan Division of Bureau of East Asian and Pacific Affairs of State Department John Malott, and National Security Advisor Brent Scowcroft. These officials unanimously insisted that financial aid was *not* enough. Scowcroft emphasized the significance of ships and airplanes that display the Japanese national flag (*Asahi Shimbun*, 1990, October 17: 1). They considered that such actions would ideally symbolize Japan's position in the world (Murata, 2008: 109–10).

In Tokyo, Ambassador Armacost elaborated on these requests. Armacost emphasized medical volunteers, logistical support in transporting personnel and equipment to Saudi Arabia, assistance in managing the exodus of refugees from Kuwait, and the dispatch of minesweepers and transport vessels to carry equipment from Egypt to Saudi Arabia. The bottom line was the deployment of *Japanese* ships staffed by *Japanese* personnel and bearing the *Japanese* flag as a symbol of Tokyo's involvement in a common endeavor with the United States. Armacost was particularly confident that the dispatch of Japanese minesweepers would contribute immensely to the coalition as the most suitable means of Japan's nonlethal activity (Armacost, 1996: 102–3).

Washington dispatched an inter-agency team of State, Defense, and National Security Council personnel to Tokyo in August. The team aimed to encourage, influence, and accelerate a Japanese decision on manpower dispatch (Armacost, 1996: 103–4). Minoru Tanba, MOFA's North American Affairs Bureau, visited the White House and DOD in late August. The United States requested that Japan provide 35 round-trip airlifts between the US mainland and eastern Saudi Arabia, where multinational coalition forces would assemble. However, Japan offered only two round trips between Japan and western Saudi Arabia, on the condition that no loading of weapons and soldiers would take place (Tanba, 2011: 75–9).

This kind of gap also served as the basis for US requests for sealifts. Japan managed to charter some normal cargo ships, but the United States requested roll-on/roll-off ships for immediate loading of soldiers, automobiles, trucks, semi-trailer trucks, trailers, and rail-road cars to Saudi Arabia. The United States desperately needed them because US forces did not possess enough of them (Teshima,

1993: 118–33; Ishihara, 1997: 66; Iokibe and Miyagi, 2013: 28–31). Some DOD officials severely blamed Tanba for this misunderstanding because Japanese tankers at that time were still transporting oil in the Persian Gulf (Tanba, 2011: 78; Teshima, 1993: 118–33; Kunimasa, 1999: 30–1; Murata, 2008: 110; Ishihara, 1997: 67). The other US physical request was to send the medical team. The Japanese Government recruited ten doctors and dispatched them to the Middle East. Nevertheless, they refused medical activities in a battlefield that was construed as unconstitutional (Ishihara, 1997: 70). Japan rejected all US physical requests in August.

These rejections of Japanese physical support steered the United States toward demanding increased financial support from Japan. Bush sent Treasury Secretary Nick Brady to Tokyo on September 7 with little advanced notice (Armacost, 1996: 107). Brady asked Japanese Finance Minister Ryūtarō Hashimoto for funding to the amount of $3 billion (Murata, 2008: 110–11), but Hashimoto was reserved in his response.[8] Brady returned home hugely disappointed (Armacost, 1996: 108; Teshima, 1993: 239–41; Kunimasa, 1999: 40–2).

Kaifu met Bush in New York on September 29. The atmosphere of their summit meeting was chilly (Murata, 2008: 112; Teshima, 1993: 154). Bush requested that Kaifu provide JSDF support for trans-portation, logistics, and medicine, without resorting to force.[9] With this pressure, Kaifu urged the passage of a United Nations Peace Cooperation (UNPC) bill that would inaugurate the United Nations Cooperation Corps (UNCC) consisting of JSDF personnel. This bill was rejected at the Diet. This bill generated fierce debate on all levels across the Japanese political spectrum, although it was able to gain support in Western countries (Reid, 1990b).

As the outbreak of the war approached, the Defense Bureau Chief of the JDA, Shigeru Hatakeyama, met Special Assistant to the President Karl Jackson and other senior officials of the US Department of Defense in Washington, DC, on January 10, 1991. They unani-mously told Hatakeyama that mere financial support was not good enough. They expressed that Japanese physical support was critically important when considering the prevalent antipathies of the American general public towards Japan (*Asahi Shimbun*, 1991, January 24, 1991: 2). Japanese Foreign Minister Nakayama visited Baker in Washington on January 14. Baker asked Nakayama for Japanese physical presence once again, referring to the fact that American citizens were now risking their lives (*Asahi Shimbun*, 1991, January 24, 1991: 2; Kunimasa, 1999: 256). On the evening of January 16 (US time), Baker informed Ambassador Murata that the multinational coalition was about to enter the war. Baker also urged Murata to make the same decision that he had requested of Nakayama.

In Tokyo, Armacost wanted to assure that Japan would provide a significant assistance package on the brink of war. He visited several key politicians and officials (Armacost, 1996: 119). Armacost visited a major factional leader of the LDP, Kiichi Miyazawa, on January 16 (Japan time). Armacost told Miyazawa that the United States wanted Japan's immediate and unambiguous decision on financial support, the transport of refugees, relief, and assistance to Gulf countries (*Asahi Shimbun*, 1991, January 24: 2). Receiving US pressure both in Washington and Tokyo, Kaifu announced on January 17 (Japanese time), the day that the US-led multinational coalition entered the war, that Japan would dispatch civilian or JSDF aircraft to evacuate war refugees from the war zone (Kunimasa, 1999: 247; *Yomiuri Shimbun*, 1991, January 17, Evening Edition: 1).

Kaifu decided to revise the enforcement ordinance based on Section 5 of Article 100 of the Self-Defense Forces Law to deploy JSDF aircraft overseas without constitutional reinterpretation. Section 5 of Article 100 refers to the transportation of state guests or others, and the cabinet decided to revise Section 16 of Article 126 by adding the word "refugees." The cabinet believed this approach would be palatable to opposition parties. Based on this legal justification, Kaifu decided to deploy JSDF Lockheed C-130 Hercules military transport aircraft because the war came to an end immediately following the decision (*Yomiuri Shmbun*, 1991, January 24: 1–2; *Asahi Shimbun*, 1991, January 24: 1). On January 24, Kaifu informed Bush of this decision (Yomiuri Shimbun, 1991, January 25: 1).[10] Murata also conveyed this decision to several key US Congressmen. They highly praised the Japanese decision to deploy its aircraft (Murata, 2008: 116).

Nevertheless, the Japanese decision on JSDF's C-130 Hercules never materialized (Murata, 2008: 118; *Asahi Shimbun*, 1991, March 1: 30). The Persian Gulf War ended on February 27. Japanese military presence in the Gulf region was completely absent during the war. Japan was cast as a liar (Murata, 2008: 118), causing Congress, the media, and the general public in the United States to become critical of Japan (Murata, 2008: 118).

Japan's unprecedented attempts for physical support continued even after the war. The Kuwaiti Government issued a one-page advertisement in the *Washington Post* on March 11 thanking 30 countries for its liberation from Iraq, including Germany but not Japan. Ambassador Murata issued an official telegram dated March 12, 1991 making a plea to send minesweepers to the Persian Gulf to clear Japan's name (Murata, 2008: 119–20).

This propelled the LDP to consider sending the SDF to the Persian Gulf. The JDA argued in support of the notion that a mission to remove underwater mines was legal under the existing Self-Defense Forces Law. If the mission was not related to combat activities, it would not be illegal even in international waters (*Asahi Shimbun*, 1991, March 16: 2). Japan's Socialist Party (JSP), Kōmeitō, and the Japan Communist Party (JCP) again opposed sending minesweepers (*Asahi Shimbun*, 1991, March 15: 2). However, business circles supported dispatching the minesweepers. The Petroleum Association of Japan, the Japanese Ship Owners Association, and the All Japan Seamen's Union unanimously urged the Japanese Government to secure safe passage in the Persian Gulf (*Asahi Shimbun*, 1991, April 11: 2).

The pressures from the LDP, DA, and business circles led Kaifu to dispatch SDF minesweepers to the Persian Gulf (Asahi Shimbun, 1991, April 12: 1, 3). The JSP, Kōmeitō, and the JCP, however, withheld their support (*Asahi Shimbun*, 1991, April 24: 1, 4). On April 24, Defense Director-General Yukihiko Ikeda ordered the deployment of six minesweepers and 500 seamen (*Asahi Shimbun*, 1991, April 25: 1). The minesweepers left for the Persian Gulf on April 26 (*Asahi Shimbun*, 1991, April 27: 30). Bush's first request to Japan to send minesweepers on August 14 of the previous year was finally granted. It took nine months. By the time the six Japanese minesweepers headed to the Persian Gulf, the war had already been over for two months.

Let us examine the course of events between Japan and the United States from August 1990 to April 1991 with the questions posed at the beginning of this chapter.

Did the United States and Japan act as partners? The answer is positive. The United States behaved as a partner of Japan from the beginning of the crisis. We saw several instances. Armacost recommended that Kaifu carry out the previously planned diplomatic tour of the Gulf nations in August. Bush specifically requested "minesweepers" when he had a telephone summit with Kaifu in August. Scowcroft and several officials from the US Department of State emphasized Japan's *symbolic* act of sending "Japan's" aircraft. Armacost also made identical requests to the State Department in August.

Japan acted as a partner of the United States throughout the Gulf crisis. Japan froze Kuwait's assets immediately after the outbreak of the crisis. Although Japan failed to achieve several symbolic actions requested by the United States, Japan undertook enormous efforts to make them possible. To make the case for aircraft dispatch in August,

Tanba visited the White House and DOD beforehand, in late August 1990. This indicates Japan's willingness to supply the United States with what it needed.

Hashimoto's rejection of Brady's financial request in Tokyo in September seems to have contradicted US expectations. Nevertheless, the Ministry of Finance (MOF) exhausted its budget, and there was no way for Hashimoto to promise a new budget as Brady had asked. Indeed, Hashimoto readily accepted Brady's identical request in January 1991.

The most notable evidence of Japan's status as a partner of the United States was its effort to pass the UNPC bill, despite stormy political battles at all levels across the political spectrum. The UNPC bill failed to pass, but Kaifu continued to seek an JSDF presence in the Persian Gulf. His effort finally succeeded in sending five JSDF minesweepers in April 1991. Personnel aids challenged Japanese postwar norms of pacifism. The challenge took place within the Kaifu Cabinet, the MOFA, and the LDP and the opposition parties. Since it challenged a nearly-half-century-old taboo, sending the SDF overseas could not be achieved as quickly as the United States had hoped. The physical presence of Japanese forces involved a number of issues, such as constitutional interpretation, legality, struggles between the MOFA and the JDA, resistance from the opposition parties, and political battles within the LDP. The JSDF dispatch was not only about a response to a US request but also about how Japan itself should be involved in international security efforts, given its rigid pacifism. Japan's behaviors were not what the US expected in terms of scope, timing, and scale; nevertheless, we have seen that Japan made significant efforts to respond to the international crisis despite its domestic political and constitutional concerns. Therefore, I believe that Japan behaved as a US partner.

Did the United States and Japan have explicit collective interests or a common good? The answer is yes. Both Japan and the United States aimed for the immediate withdrawal of Iraqi forces from Kuwait. The immediate US deployment of its armed forces and Japan's freezing of Kuwait's assets immediately following the Iraqi invasion exemplified their united idea of rejecting Iraqi military and political intentions. Although Japan's attempt at physical assistance failed, it repeatedly tried to achieve it. This was also the case with Japanese Finance Minister Hashimoto's agreement with US Treasury Secretary Brady to provide additional financial assistance of $9 billion in January 1991, even when it resulted in a tax increase for Japan. Japan's financial support demonstrated its national interest in liberating Kuwait.

Did the United States and Japan have collective strategic perspectives? The answer is mixed. Japan seemed to understand US intentions to generate a "new world order" through the Persian Gulf War, as Bush had advocated in his speech at the US Congress. Japan made an enormous effort to contribute to the US victory with all available means. Nevertheless, it is questionable whether Japan was fully aware of what the United States needed for its initial deployment of armed forces. The dispatch of Japanese DA officer Tanba to the Pentagon in August exemplified this. In August, the United States needed transportation for US forces in Europe for dispatch to Saudi Arabia; otherwise, the initially deployed US forces would collapse following an invasion of Iraq into Saudi Arabia. Tanba directly confirmed this critical status of US military deployment in Saudi Arabia.

However, these actions are at the level of tactics rather than strategy. Strategy is a higher form of statecraft than tactics. According to British strategic thinker Liddell Hart, while tactics are the application of the military instrument that translate into actual fighting, deployment, and control, the main concerns of strategy are the movement of forces, their roles, and outcomes (Hart, 1967: 335–6). Following Hart's argument, Japan was not able to be directly concerned with the operational level of armed forces but indirectly affected the course of US military actions through the country's vast financial aid. Therefore, Japan may have shared the strategic outlook of the US.

Did the shared collective strategic perspectives of the United States and Japan influence the process and outcome of the deliberations? This study showed that it did. Both countries exchanged their views on the war through various channels. Armacost's activities in Tokyo and Murata's activities in Washington, meetings between Brady and Hashimoto, and a number of related agencies and ministries in both countries were held to share strategic perspectives.

These interactions significantly influenced the Japanese policy-making process. The Defense Agency was actively involved in Japan's security policy-making for the first time in postwar Japanese politics.[11] Since the MOFA was the main agency for national security policy throughout the postwar period, DA participation in the UNPC bill during October–November 1990 represented a significant change. This finally led to the first JSDF overseas dispatch in April 1991. Furthermore, this change also evolved into Japan's participation in United Nations peacekeeping operations (PKOs) on a regular basis, which became a major mission of the SDF in later years. "The Gulf shock" led Japan to rethink its international role. Some argue that Japan was dramatically transformed into a "normative power."[12]

Conclusion

This chapter examined the Persian Gulf War from August 2, 1990 to April 26, 1991 to confirm US-Japan collective identity, which is an essential part of their bilateral security community. Following Cronin's verification method, this study examined the discourse and behavior during the period. The results were as follows.

In the discourse analysis, discrepancies were found between the two countries. Japan's reference to international contribution is more general than US recognition of its involvement in international security. While the United States specifically used terms such as "minesweepers," "Japanese flag," or "roll-on/roll-off" cargo ships, the Japanese idea was vague, UN-based, and less specific than that of the United States. This discrepancy continued until the end of the war. Japan's frequent use of the term "contribution (*kōken*)" exemplifies its basic state of mind regarding the war. Despite such a discrepancy, the United States and Japan spoke of themselves as part of the same social group aligned against Saddam Hussein. The discourse informs us that the recognition discrepancy was not serious enough to threaten their sense of belonging to the same group opposing the "Hitler-like" Iraqi dictator.

Regarding behavioral analysis, this article raised four questions. Did the United States and Japan act as partners? Did the United States and Japan have explicit collective interests or common goals? Did the United States and Japan have collective strategic perspectives? Did the shared collective strategic perspectives of the US and Japan influence the process and outcome of the deliberations? While answers to the first, second, and fourth questions are positive, the answer to the third question is mixed. This confirmation informs us of the possibility of a security community between Japan and the United States, although further case studies are required.

Notes

1 Adler and Barnett argue that the final stage of a security community's evolution is Phase III, "mature," in which collective identity appears and in which altruism can be seen among member states. See Emanuel Adler and Michael Barnett, "A framework for the study of security community," in *Security Communities*, edited by Adler and Barnett (Cambridge: Cambridge University Press, 1998), 37–58.

2 The five principles are (1) mutual respect for sovereignty and territorial integrity, (2) mutual nonaggression, (3) noninterference in each other's internal affairs, (4) equality and mutual benefit, and (5) peaceful coexistence. See

Hwei-ling Huo, "Patterns of Behavior in China's Foreign Policy: The Gulf Crisis and Beyond," *Asian Survey* 32(3) (March 1992): 269.

3 According to an interview with Ozawa conducted by a Japanese journalist Takeshige Kunimasa, Ozawa emphasized the importance of alignment with the United States because it was the only way for Japan to survive in the world. See Takeshige Kunimasa, *Wangan Sensō to yū Tenkaiten: Dōten Suru Nihon Seiji* (Tokyo: Iwanami Shoten, 1999), 90.

4 The "pacifist" identity refers to a granting of great importance to nonmilitary means of achieving peace. It prefers the preservation of Article 9 as a symbol of Japanese pacifism and demands the dissolution of the SDF as well the US-Japan alliance because of their unconstitutionality. A "pragmatic multilateralist" insists that Japan should emphasize increasing relations with Asia while maintaining an alliance with the United States. The "centrist" stresses the importance of national interests based on a zero-sum view of world politics. See also Susanne Kline, *Rethinking Japan's Identity and International Role: An Intercultural Perspective* (London: Routledge, 2002).

5 For this project, Kaifu consulted with a number of people. These were former Japanese Ambassador to the US Nobuo Matsunaga, the chairman of SONY, Akio Morita, Honor Advisor of Itochu Corporation Ryūzō Sejima, and Tokai University professor Kenzō Uchida. See Kunimasa (1999: 62–4).

6 Although he tried to avoid getting involved in the legislative process, Armacost was characterized by the Japanese media as having pressured the Japanese government. See Armacost (1996: 115–18).

7 Baker never specified the scope of further contribution from Japan. A Japanese journalist, Ryūichi Teshima, interpreted it as a merely financial contribution. See Teshima (1993: 230–1).

8 Hashimoto explained later that the MOF exhausted all reserved funds as Brady came to Japan in September 1990; therefore, the MOF was simply unable to prepare a new budget. Hashimoto also blamed the MOFA for not sharing information on US financial requests with the MOF in advance. For a detailed account, see Iokibe and Miyagi (2013: 34–5).

9 Bush's term *Japanese force* clearly means the Japan Self-Defense Force. See *Asahi Shimbun* (1990, October 16: 1); Kunimasa (1999: 61–2); Teshima (1993: 154).

10 During a G7 meeting in New York, Japanese Minister of Finance Ryūtarō Hashimoto held a bilateral ministerial meeting with US Treasury Secretary Brady at the Stanhope Hotel, New York on January 20. Brady explained that the war would be costly because it would require massive air attacks for a long period using expensive Tomahawk Missiles and smart bombs. Brady asked Hashimoto to finance $9 billion of the war. Hashimoto readily agreed. See Iokibe and Miyagai (2013: 37–43); Teshima (1993: 265–8); Murata (2008: 115–16); Kunimasa (1999: 271–2); Ishihara (1997: 71–3).

11 There was a similar case in the 1980s. Under Nakasone Yasuhiro's Premiership, the JDA advocated defense enhancement to contribute to the Western defense camp's total defense efforts. This influenced policymaking with respect to the defense budget. See Yoshimasa Muroyama,

Nichibei Anpo Taisei: Reisengo no Anzen Hoshō Senryaku wo Kōsō Suru: Nixon Doctrine Kara Wangan Sensō Made (Tokyo: Yūikaku, 1992b), 480–1.

12 Rok Zupančič and Miha Hribernik argue that after the Persian Gulf War, Japan has become a "normative power" that *promotes* certain norms of global life through diplomacy and security activities, including UN peacekeeping operations. See: Rok Zupančič and Miha Hribernik, " 'Discovering' Normative Power as a State Strategy in the Framework of Saecurity, Foreign, and Defense Policy: The Case of Japan," *Philippine Political Science Journal* 35(1) (2014): 79; Rok Zupančič, "Normative Power Japan: The European Union's Ideational Successor or Another 'Contribution in Terms'?" *Romanian Journal of Political Science* (December 2013): 119. Emilian Kavalski made a similar argument; see Emilian Kavalski, "The Shadows of Normative Power in Asia: Framing the International Agency of China, India and Japan," *Pacific Focus* 29(3) (December 2014): 303–28.

4 Nurturing Collective Identity
The September 11 Terrorist Attacks (2001)

Introduction

This chapter will examine political interactions between Japan and the United States from September 11, 2001, when the Islamic extremist group al-Qaeda, led by Osama bin Laden, attacked the World Trade Center in New York and the Pentagon in Washington, DC, to October 29, 2001, when the Anti-Terrorism Special Measures Law was overwhelmingly approved at the Japanese Diet. The September 11 terrorist attacks killed at least 3,000 people. To assist US forces' retaliatory attack against bin Laden and his assumed protector the Taliban in Afghanistan in the name of Operation Enduring Freedom, Japan swiftly passed the law that enabled it to send three JSDF warships to Diego Garcia in the Indian Ocean.

In the 1990s, the US-Japan alliance developed significantly. The Persian Gulf War opened the doorway to the JSDF's overseas dispatch. This process was accelerated with the passage of the Act on Cooperation with United Nations Peacekeeping Operations in 1992 that enabled JSDF to assume UN peacekeeping operation (PKO) missions around the globe. JSDF's overseas dispatch became no longer a taboo for Japanese politics, even though full-scale military activities remained severely limited. Further institutional development of the alliance with the Nye Initiatives (the East Asian Security Review) of 1995 reconfirmed the importance of the alliance and the maintenance of 100,000 US soldiers stationed in the East Asian region. Japan revised its National Defense Program Outline (NDPO) in 1995 after its 20 years of enforcement to adapt to a post-Cold War environment. These efforts were integrated into the US-Japan Joint Declaration on Security of 1996 that expressed the country's bilateral cooperation for international security *beyond* East Asia. The alliance also revised the Guidelines for the US-Japan Defense Cooperation in 1997. Morimoto

(1997) evaluated this series of institutional changes as "the most significant turning point for the alliance since the 1960 Mutual Security Treaty." Finally, Japan enacted the Law on a Situation in the Areas Surrounding Japan and amended the Self-Defense Forces Law and the Agreement Concerning the Reciprocal Provision of Logistic Support, Supplies, and Services (ACSA) in 1999.

Despite these institutional developments, the September 11 terrorist attacks generated another trial for the country's relationship simply because the alliance was never designed to cope with terrorism. The series of institutional developments in the 1990s were *not* sufficiently effective to counter global terrorism. To assist the United States, Japan inevitably needed to employ the concept of collective self-defense because Japanese soil was *not* attacked. Nevertheless, the traditional interpretation of Japan's constitution, Article 9 does not allow Japan to exercise this concept. The September 11 terrorist attacks provide an important case for detecting the collective identity of the United States and Japan in such institutionally unprepared circumstances in terms of how they spoke and behaved.

Puzzles

Unlike during the Persian Gulf War (1990–1), after September 11, Japan quickly enacted laws enabling JMSDF ships to deploy in the Indian Ocean to operate with US forces. The United States held Japan's swift legislation and its decision on the JMSDF joining the US "War on Terror" in high regard. This was one of the most dramatic events post-September 11 for Northeast Asian security (Gill, 2002: 44). Why did Japan act so quickly? There are several possible answers.

Domestic institutional factors could account for it. Domestic institutional reforms in the 1990s changed the decision-making process in Japanese politics. The election reform of 1994 enabled Koizumi to form his own powerful cabinet in April 2001 without relying on the traditionally factional politics that allocated ministerial positions based on seniority rather than ambition and creativity (Arase, 2007). Kabashima and Steel (2007) also pointed out that Koizumi benefited from changes in the Liberal Democratic Party (LDP). Koizumi's skill of making politics into entertainment using the media accelerated his high popularity. His cabinet support rate was nearly 70 percent around September 11 (Kabashima and Steel, 2007: 81). Furthermore, a strengthened Cabinet Secretariat as the core executive within the Prime Minister's Official Residence (PMOR) made it possible for Koizumi to be able to exercise "top-down" diplomacy centered within the PMOR (Shinoda, 2005).

The Koizumi government was also able to bypass prior consultation with the LDP while making post-September 11 policies (Shinoda, 2004: 57).

However, these domestic institutional accounts are only partially persuasive. International factors must be considered because such Japanese security measures might have offended its Asian neighbors. Midford (2003) discussed this factor. Midford first pointed out that although Koizumi held his powerful leadership with wide public support, coalition partner Komeito continued to resist. Koizumi did not have a free hand to devise security policies entirely (Midford, 2003: 338). Rather, the near absence of Asian countries' pressures on Japan not to dispatch its JSDF overseas made Koizumi's decision easy. Japan's past record on "benign" security activities, i.e., United Nations peacekeeping operation missions in the 1990s, reassured Asian countries into accepting Japan's new security roles (Midford, 2003).

These explanations are partial. Domestic accounts do not explain why the Japanese public *still* supported Koizumi widely when he devised an unprecedented military involvement in the War on Terror that was more radical than the Persian Gulf War. Likewise, the international account of the absence of Asian pressure does not explain why the Japanese Government wanted to cooperate with the United States in the first place. Instead, it explains why Japan *was able* to do it rather than why Japan *did* it. Both explanations describe only conditions rather than the government's impulse. Conditions solely cannot determine behaviors. Unless we closely examine whether there was a sense of "we-feeling" (liberal anti-terrorists) and "others" (terrorists), our understanding of Japan's behaviors in the post-September 11 period remains incomplete.

The September 11 Terrorist Attacks

Discourse

Koizumi entered the Prime Minister's Official Residence (PMOR) at approximately 22:00, when Taro Aso, Chairman of the Liberal Democratic Party (LDP)'s Research Council, ran into the residence. Aso said to Koizumi, "There has been no case in which the US mainland was attacked, ever in its history. After the Cold War, we must prepare to deal with terrorism. The axis of Japan's foreign policy will be how we go along with the United States. It will be tough for Japan" (*Yomiuri Shimbun Seijibu*, 2006: 124). Around that time, the Japan Maritime Self-Defense Force's (JMSDF's) Chief of Staff, Tōru Ishikawa, made a phone call to the Commander of the US Navy in Japan, Robert Chaplin.

Chaplin said, "This is war!" and Ishikawa replied, "JMSDF will provide as much assistance to the United States as possible" (Yomiuri *Shimbun Seijibu*, 2006: 124).

Indeed, Koizumi expressed his unconditional support to the United States immediately after the incident. This tone was quite consistent until the United States entered into a retaliatory attack on Afghanistan. Koizumi stated,

> The series of terrorist attacks that occurred yesterday in the United States of America took a great number of precious lives. These extremely vicious acts of violence can never be forgiven. I am outraged by these acts which pose a grave challenge not only to the United States but to the entire free world ... Japan strongly supports the United States and is resolved to spare no effort in providing necessary assistance and cooperation. We must firmly together with the concerned nations of the world to ensure that such acts are never repeated.
>
> (Prime Minister of Japan and His Cabinet, 2001, September 12)

Koizumi sent an identical message to Bush on the phone on September 13. As a partner in the coalition government, Komeito also impeached the terrorism as "a serious challenge to peace and democracy" (*Asahi Shimbun*, 2001, September 12, Evening Edition: 8). Both the Japanese Ministry of Foreign Affairs (MOFA) and the Japan Defense Agency (JDA) uniformly expressed their strong support for the United States (*Asahi Shimbun*, 2001, September 12, Evening Edition: 8). Gen Nakatani, JDA Director General, said at the government ruling party's liaison meeting on September 12, "Under the current laws, the JSDF cannot protect US military bases in Japan. It is still exclusively under the jurisdiction of the National Police Agency. Therefore, please hurry up and revise this law" (*Asahi Shimbun*, 2001, September 13: 4).

The most renowned phrase of the post-September 11 discourse was "show the flag." The media widely attributed the phrase to US Deputy Secretary of State Richard Armitage (*Asahi Shimbun*, 2001, September 20: 4), but it originated with John Hill, the US Defense Department's Chief of Division of Japan. Hill told the Japanese Envoy to the United States Ichirō Komatsu by phone, "The United States will take actions soon. Japan will be surely asked for help. Please raise the Rising-Sun flag" (*Yomiuri Shimbun Seijibu*, 2006: 127–8). Former US Deputy Assistant Defense Secretary Kurt Campbell met the Japanese Defense Agency's Director-General of the Secretariat Takemasa Moriya in Tokyo on September 14. Campbell gave advice to Moriya: "The most important thing is that Japan makes a voluntary and visible assistance policy at the right time" (*Yomiuri Shimbun Seijibu*, 2006: 127). On September 15, Armitage had a short meeting with the Japanese Ambassador to the United States, Shunji Yanai, in Washington, DC. Armitage said, "I will say this to you as your friend. To avoid creating political devastation like the Persian Gulf War, Japan needs to announce visibly specific polices that can show the Rising Sun flag and faces of Japanese people" (*Yomiuri Shimbun Seijibu*, 2006: 127; Hisae, 2002: 23–4). Armitage emphasized the significance of prompt actions (Hisae, 2002: 24).

Interestingly, Armitage made it clear that the United States understood Japan's constitutional constraints. The JSDF did not have to participate in combat activities. Armitage said, "Japan can do many things for logistic support. You can think of various things, but basically, you can load anything. I believe that Japan will be highly appreciated by us if the Japanese government formally announces to assist transport of US forces by JMSDF ships or Japan Air Self-Defense Force's (JASDF) aircrafts. The United States highly respects Japan for their actions" (Hisae, 2002: 24).

Armitage wanted to avoid a situation like the Persian Gulf War of 1990–1, in which Japan was criticized for being an automatic teller machine because Japan simply sent checks without human participation (*Yomiuri Shimbun Seijibu*, 2006: 127). Yanai shared this feeling. Yanai was traumatized that the International Peace Cooperation Bill was rejected at the Diet during the Persian Gulf Crisis. Yanai was convinced that "Japan needs to begin visible assistance to US wars against terrorism" (*Yomiuri Shimbun Seijibu*, 2006: 127).

"Show the flag" became a flashback to the bitter memory of the Persian Gulf War of 1990–1 among officials of the MOFA and JDA (Hisae, 2002: 26–7). Therefore, the MOFA immediately recognized a need for new legislation enabling the JSDFs to cooperate with US forces, which is "the last test of the US-Japan alliance" (*Asahi Shimbun*, 2001, September 20: 2). To "show the flag" then transformed into symbolic terms representing the US's high expectations for Japan's human participation. It also played a major role in growing anti-terrorist sentiments among the Japanese public to the point that Japan must take action. This movement reduced social obstacles to the JSDF overseas dispatch (Hisae, 2002: 27).

On September 19, before announcing the seven anti-terrorism specific measures, Koizumi stated,

I am filled with overwhelming indignation at the terrorist attacks in the United States, which represent attacks not only on the United

States but attacks on freedom, peace and democracy of the whole of humankind. Recognizing this, I was resolved for Japan to take its own initiative towards the eradication of terrorism, in cooperation with the United States and other countries concerned.

(Prime Minister of Japan and His Cabinet, 2001, September 19).

Specific anti-terrorism measures were the following.

(1) The Government of Japan (GOJ) will promptly take measures necessary for dispatching the Self-Defense Force (SDF) for providing support—including medical services, transportation and supplies—to the US forces and others taking measures related to the terrorist attacks, which have been recognized as a threat to international peace and security in the United Nations Security Council Resolution 1368.
(2) The GOJ will promptly take measures necessary to further strengthen the protection of facilities and areas of the US forces and important facilities in Japan.
(3) The GOJ will swiftly dispatch SDF vessels to gather information.
(4) The GOJ will strengthen international cooperation, including information sharing, in areas such as immigration control.
(5) The GOJ will extend humanitarian, economic, and other necessary assistance to surrounding and affected countries. As a part of this assistance, the GOJ will extend emergency economic assistance to Pakistan and India, which are cooperating with the United States in this emergency situation.
(6) The GOJ will provide assistance to displaced persons as necessary. This action will include the possibility of humanitarian assistance by SDF.
(7) The GOJ, in cooperation with other countries, will take appropriate measures in response to the changing situation to avoid confusion in the international and domestic economic systems.

(Prime Minister of Japan and His Cabinet, 2001, September 19).

Koizumi became a part of the G8 joint statement, as follows.

We, the leaders of the G8, condemn in the strongest terms the barbaric acts of terrorism carried out against the United States of America on September 11. Our condolences do not end at America's borders, for New York and Washington are international cities where many nationalities have made their homes. The perpetrators—and all who have harbored, assisted or supported them by any means—have launched an offensive against innocent persons and against the central values and interests of the international community. Their actions constitute a profound threat to the peace, prosperity, and security of all people, of all faiths, of every nation. We will not allow those who perpetrate hatred and terror to divide the peoples and cultures of the world.

(Prime Minister of Japan and His Cabinet, 2001, September 20)

Koizumi then stated at the Ceremony for All Victims of Terrorist Attacks in the US that was held in the Tokyo Big Sight in Tokyo on September 23:

These terrorist attacks are a serious challenge not only to the United States, but to the freedom, peace and democracy of the world … There is an expression: "A friend in need is a friend indeed." In the fight against terrorism and in the effort to assist the victims, the people of all nations of the world, including the United States, must combine their efforts in cooperation. I am resolved to work hand in hand with the nations of the world to build a peaceful international community that is free of terrorism.

(Prime Minister of Japan and His Cabinet, 2001, September 23)

These prime minister's statements contained the words "freedom," "peace," and "democracy," in contrast to "terrorism" and "barbaric acts." Such a contrast was used elsewhere when the prime minister's statement was released in the post-September 11 period. To affirm this contrast, the US-Japan community of practice spelled out "promptly take measures necessary" only six days after the terrorist attacks. In so doing, Japan and the United States revealed Osama bin Laden and his collaborators to be "others."

Koizumi abruptly visited New York on September 24. He went straight to Ground Zero (Iijima, 2007: 29–31). Koizumi remarked in his own English at the joint press conference with New York Mayor Rudolph Giuliani that Japan would be with the United States to fight against terrorism. Koizumi also said, "I am so grateful that Japanese residents here have been warmly helped by New Yorkers." These remarks were received favorably by US press (Iijima, 2006: 126–7; Iijima, 2007: 30–1).

Koizumi met Bush in Washington, DC on September 25. Koizumi said, "This terrorism is not just someone else's problem. I believe this is also Japan's problem. We must respond to terrorism proactively" (Hisae, 2002: 48). Koizumi continued, "Japan will help the United States. To fight against terrorism, it requires determination and patience." Bush said, "Our mission is to eradicate international terrorism." Koizumi then said, "I stand by you. I will help you, Mr. President." Bush repeatedly said to Koizumi, "Thank you" (*Yomiuri Shimbun Seijibu*, 2006: 134).

Koizumi told Bush that Japan was now preparing to provide non-combat logistic support to US forces. Bush replied that the United States regarded such efforts by Japan highly. He also made clear that Japan would not be degraded by Japan's decision not to send combatants (*Asahi Shimbun*, 2001, September 26, Evening Edition: 1). Bush repeated this when he met Koizumi again at the APEC meeting in Shanghai in October (*Asahi Shimbun*, 2001, October 21: 1, 4).

Koizumi and Bush made a statement expressing explicit identity sharing. Bush remarked that

> all the Japanese people must understand that the United States was fighting against evil people who hate freedom and that it was time to stand together and fight against terrorism.
>
> (Hisae, 2002: 49)

During the summit meeting with Bush, Koizumi made clear his intention to fight with the United States against terrorists (Iijima, 2006: 127; Hisae, 2002: 48). Bush and Koizumi explicitly expressed the determination shared by the two national leaders at a joint press conference. Bush was asked by a Japanese press reporter, "According to a public opinion survey, 90% of the Japanese people are afraid of becoming a target for terrorists if they support US military actions. What do you think of that?" Bush became sullen with him and said

> Japanese people should understand that we are now fighting against evil people who hate freedom … It is time to stand up and fight together against terrorism. We must not let terrorists do as they want. It is a fight between good and evil, and Prime Minister Koizumi understands it. I believe the Japanese people do, too.
>
> (Hisae, 2002: 49)

Koizumi then stated emotionally, "We support the US fight against terrorism. We must fight with patience and determination to achieve the goal of crushing terrorism at the global level" (Hisae, 2002: 49).

Former Assistant Secretary of State for East Asian and Pacific Affairs during the Clinton Administration, Kurt Campbell, commented on this summit: "this summit was entirely different from past summits that were only pretense. I am impressed by their sincerity on tackling issues. It was a breakthrough for US-Japanese relations" (*Asahi Shimbun*, 2001, September 27: 4).

Koizumi repeatedly expressed this shared identity when he returned to Japan. He stated in his general policy speech at the Diet on September 27, "the multiple terrorist attacks that occurred in the United States were attacks against not only the United States but also humanity. As I visited the site of terrorist attacks, I once again felt strong indignation against such inhuman behaviors" (*Asahi Shimbun*, 2001, September 27, Evening Edition: 3). US Undersecretary of State John Bolton said that Japan's response so far has been "very active" (*Asahi Shimbun*, 2001, October 6: 7). On October 8, when US forces began military strikes against the Taliban regime in Afghanistan, Koizumi stated the following at his press conference:

> International terrorism is a despicable act that threatens the lives and lifestyles of people all over the world and the peace and security of all the countries in the world. Right now, an overwhelming number of the countries of the world, irrespective of differences on other issues, are united in condemning and fighting against inhumane acts of terrorism. Japan strongly supports the actions by the United States and other countries to prevent and eradicate international terrorism, and will provide all possible cooperation. I have already conveyed these positions of Japan to President Bush in our telephone conversation early this morning. Japan regards the fight against terrorism as its own challenge, and has been taking effective counter-measures on its own initiatives.
>
> (Prime Minister of Japan and His Cabinet, 2001, October 8)

This statement revealed Koizumi's dichotomy of good and evil. The "inhuman" terrorism threatens "the lives and lifestyles of the people all over the world and the peace and security of all the countries in the world" that connotes Western values such as freedom, democracy, and peace. This statement contained a phrase—"the fight against terrorism as its own challenge"—that clearly indicates Japan's sense of belonging to the anti-terrorist camp.

Koizumi then issued a statement regarding the passage of the Anti-Terrorism Special Measures bill in the Diet on October 29 as follows.

> We now need to implement our response based on the new law as soon as possible. The Government now initiates necessary considerations and coordination with other concerned countries and parties to expeditiously compile a Basic Plan in accordance with

this law and makes preparations to ensure that response measures be promptly implemented after the compilation of the Basic Plan.

The Government views the fight against terrorism as a challenge of its own, and will take measures based upon this law proactively and of its own initiative within the framework of international cooperation, with a view to securing the safety of the nation and its people. Measures aiming for the eradication of terrorism, including measures based on amendments to the Self-Defense Forces Law and the Japan Coast Guard Law, will be comprehensively advanced, and full efforts will continue to be devoted to countering terrorism within Japan.

(Prime Minister of Japan and His Cabinet, 2001, October 29)

This statement affirmed Japan's recognition of the importance of "prompt" actions and taking an anti-terrorist stance. Newly appointed Japanese Ambassador to the United States Ryōzō Katō visited Bush in November. Bush remarked, "I am feeling friendship and support from the government and people of Japan. The US-Japan relationship is at the best time" (*Asahi Shimbun*, 2001, November 9, Evening Edition: 2). Bush visited Japan in February 2002. He made a speech at the Diet. Bush emphasized the "strength of the US-Japan alliance" and "Japan's worldwide indispensable role" (*Asahi Shimbun*, 2002, February 19, Evening Edition: 1). Bush answered Asahi Shimbun's question in his interview as follows.

ASAHI SHIMBUN: What do you think of Japan's anti-terrorism assistance so far?

BUSH: It has been great. This started from my personal friendship with Prime Minister Junichiro Koizumi. He is an approachable person. I am looking forward to seeing him. He said to me that he would stand by us America as a friend. He did everything that he promised to me such as sending destroyers and reconstruction assistance to Afghanistan.

(*Asahi Shimbun*, 2002, February 16, Evening Edition: 2)

Behaviors

The Japanese Government took prompt actions immediately after the terrorism. The PMOR created its liaison office collecting information on the terrorism within one-and-a-half hours after the first terrorist attack by the hijacked American Airlines aircraft (AA11) on the World Trade Center (*Asahi Shimbun*, 2001, September 12: 37; *Asahi Shimbun*,

2001, September 13: 7). Koizumi ordered Koji Omi, Minster of Science and Technology, and Minister of State for Okinawa and Northern Territories Affairs, who just happened to be in Boston for his official trip, to go to New York immediately (Prime Minister of Japan and His Cabinet, 2001, September 12). After observing the devastating crime scene at the World Trade Center, Omi urged Koizumi on the phone to call Bush immediately (*Yomiuri Shimbun Seijibu*, 2006: 126). Koizumi also assembled the government-ruling party's liaison meeting on the same day. The JDA and the National Police Agency strengthened its guard on all US military bases in Japan (*Asahi Shimbun*, 2001, September 12, Evening Edition: 8; *Asahi Shimbun*, 2001, September 13: 7). Gen Nakatani, Director General of the JDA, gave an order of the highest precaution to the Ground, Maritime and Air Self-Defense Forces (*Asahi Shimbun*, 2001, September 12, Evening Edition: 3). Nakatani was in East Timor at the time but returned to Japan immediately after the terrorist attacks. He came to the PMOR early the next morning (Iijima, 2006: 124). Nakatani then took the leadership step of revising the Self-Defense Law to enhance the security of US military bases in Japan (*Asahi Shimbun*, 2001, September 16: 4).

Chief Cabinet Secretary Yasuo Fukuda, Deputy Chief Cabinet Secretary Shinzo Abe, Kosei Ueno, and the Chairman of the LDP Research Council Taro Aso rushed into the PMOR immediately after the terrorist attacks. Specialists in emergency rescues, fire fighting, and medical treatment from various ministries and agencies thronged to the PMOR one after another. In addition, the PMOR was overly crowded with many bureau chief-class bureaucrats and party cadres, and the situation became out of control (Iijima, 2006: 122).

The center of the discussion was how the JSDF dispatch becomes feasible within constitutional constraints. The PMOR was confident that the Bush Administration would take immediate countermeasures through military action. The PMOR needed to emphasize quick actions. Shinoda (2004: 54) points out that Koizumi's prominent leadership was inevitable because Foreign Minister Makiko Tanaka caused political blunders such as divulging the US State Department's emergency evacuation location to the press and abruptly canceling a visit to Pakistan. The MOFA then malfunctioned so it was not fast enough to respond to the September 11 terrorist attacks. Koizumi decided to keep Tanaka out of the decision-making process.

The Japanese Government was traumatized by its humiliating experience in the Persian Gulf War of 1990–1, with the insulting phrase "too little, too late" used to describe Japanese assistance to the United States. Hence, the key was prompt actions. The whole of the Japanese

Government was firmly determined not to repeat its "slow" decision (Shinoda, 2006: 34). Indeed, 45 minutes after the attacks, the PMOR liaison office was launched within the CMC. Within the next hour, as the Japanese Government learned the seriousness of the terrorism, it was upgraded to the PMOR Countermeasures Headquarters (Shinoda, 2006: 34). While the mission of the liaison office is only to gather information, Countermeasures Headquarters can call up "an emergent assembling team" from concerned ministries and can support activities for those ministries (Shinoda, 2006: 34).

The very next morning, Koizumi summoned the Security Council for the first time after the North Korean Taepo-dong missile firing in 1998. Koizumi canceled his official trips to Southeast Asian countries to concentrate on the prompt actions (Prime Minister of Japan and His Cabinet, 2001, September 13). Deputy Chief Cabinet Secretary Sadajiro Furukawa held a series of secret meetings with director-general-class bureaucrats from September 13. Deputy Chief Cabinet Secretary Keiji Omori; Deputy Chief Cabinet Secretary Kazuyoshi Urabe; Shotaro Taniuchi, Chief of the MOFA Foreign Policy Bureau; Ichiro Fuzisaki, Chief of the MOFA North American Affairs Bureau; Ken Sato, Administrative Vice Chief of DA; Shingo Sato, Chief of the DA Defense Policy Bureau; and Osamu Akiyama, Vice Chief of the Cabinet Legislation Bureau, were present (Shinoda, 2004: 54–5).

Osamu Tsuno, Chief of the Cabinet Legislation Bureau, said at the beginning of the meetings, "We will not be quick enough to assist the United States if we use the usual process in which the Cabinet Legislation Bureau examines bills after each ministry creates them. From the beginning, the Cabinet Legislation Bureau must be present" (*Yomiuri Shimbun Seijibu*, 2006: 133). Tsuno said, "Let us assemble counselors who are above the level of division chief." Furukawa replied, "This means that counselors will represent the Chief of the Cabinet Legislation Bureau, doesn't it?" Tsuno recoiled and called on Akiyama, the Vice Chief of the Cabinet Legislation Bureau (*Yomiuri Shimbun Seijibu*, 2006: 133).

Furukawa said, "Let's brainstorm on what we can do under the existing laws, such as the Law on a Situation in the Areas Surrounding Japan or the UNPKO Cooperation Law" (*Yomiuri Shimbun Seijibu*, 2006: 133–4). The PMOR quickly concluded that the present laws could not respond to terrorism and that new laws were required. Furukawa delivered this judgment to Prime Minister Koizumi on September 15 (*Yomiuri Shimbun Seijibu*, 2006: 133).

Koizumi publicly announced at a press conference on September 19 that his government was seeking new laws and would provide the seven anti-terrorism-specific measures.[1] Koizumi decided to send emergency assistant corps to the United States at a meeting of the Security Council (*Asahi Shimbun*, 2001, September 12, Evening Edition: 3). This decision was cancelled since the United States told Japan that it is was not necessary (*Asahi Shimbun*, 2001, September 13, Evening Edition: 2). Nevertheless, Koizumi prepared *new* laws to enable the JSDF to provide logistical support to US and multinational forces (*Asahi Shimbun*, 2001, September 18: 2). The United States highly appreciated such a quick response, and the White House issued a press release expressing its gratitude (Shinoda, 2004: 57).

The government and the ruling parties (the LDP and the Komeito) met together to craft the bill concerning threats against international peace and security on September 19 (*Asahi Shimbun*, 2001, September 19, Evening Edition: 1). The DA held an urgent conference assembling cadres of the Land, Maritime and Air Self-Defense Forces to discuss the scope of their deployments on the same day (*Asahi Shimbun*, 2001, September 20: 39). The provisional name of the bill was the "Law on cooperation with the United States in accordance with United Nations Charter's Article 25 and United Nations Security Council's Resolution on International Terrorism occurring in the United States" (*Asahi Shimbun*, 2001, September 20: 1).[2]

The seven anti-terrorism-specific measures are noteworthy and were announced on September 19 *before* legislation of the new laws. Four of the seven measures were to be operated by the JSDF. The first item was JSDF's logistical support to US forces for medical, transportation, and supplies.[3] The JDA soon started organizing "the JMSDF support fleet" composed of transport ships, destroyers, and P-3C Orion anti-submarine/maritime surveillance aircrafts. This fleet possessed combat capabilities, and such a formation was the first ever attempt for the JSDF in its history (*Asahi Shimbun*, 2001, September 20: 1). The JDA also tried to sail "the JMSDF support fleet" to join the US Navy *without* legislation as soon as possible (*Asahi Shimbun*, 2001, September 25: 1).

The JDA had already entered into substantial "collective defense" with the United States. US aircraft carrier *Kitty Hawk*, accompanied by two JMSDF destroyers, left from Yokosuka on September 21 for retaliatory military operations (*Asahi Shimbun*, 2001, September 21: 1). This was Japan's response to the US request. The US Navy was afraid of being attacked by terrorists using civilian aircrafts or small boats. The defense circle of the United States and Japan recognized an aircraft carrier as a symbol of power. If the aircraft carrier were attacked, it would create a larger negative impact on the world than the fall of the World Trade Center. In addition, Japan considered that CNN's press coverage of *Kitty Hawk* being escorted by Japanese destroyers could promote a good image of Japan among the American public. Indeed, the US Government later expressed its deep appreciation on this matter to Japan (*Yomiuri Shimbun Seijibu*, 2006: 135).

After World War II, the overseas dispatch of the JSDFs was taboo. It was a turning point for Japanese security policy when the United Nations Peacekeeping Operations Law (UNPKO Law) that enabled the JSDFs to engage in security activities in the post-conflict areas was passed in 1992. Yet terrorism was outside of an assumed situation in the UNPKO Law. For this reason, the JMSDF insisted on the application of the Law on a Situation in the Areas Surrounding Japan to the September 11 attack, but the MOFA argued that the Indian Ocean could hardly be seen as "the areas surrounding Japan" (*Yomiuri Shimbun Seijibu*, 2006: 132; Hisae, 2002: 8–92). After fierce debate, the Koizumi government concluded that new laws were required to make it possible (Iijima, 2006: 122–6). Former Prime Minister Keizo Obuchi had already made a statement in 1999 that the Law on a Situation in the Areas Surrounding Japan, established in 1998, could not apply to the Middle East, the Indian Ocean, or the other side of the world. This statement became the major obstacle for the attempt to apply the Law on a Situation to September 11 (Hisae, 2002: 92–3). Therefore, Koizumi deliberately maintained an existing constitutional interpretation so his government could avoid endless debates nationwide (Shinoda, 2006: 34–5).

After the US-Japan summit on September 25, US expectation on Japan's military cooperation increased since the United States requested the dispatch of Japan's aegis destroyers because the US forces were on the alert for the recurrence of suicide bombing by hijacked aircrafts. The aegis destroyer possesses a high-end radar system capable of detecting 200 different airborne objects within a 500-km radius and intercepting them with its own missiles. MOFA was positive about this idea. MOFA considered the aegis dispatch as wide appeal for the United States (*Yomiuri Shimbun Seijibu*, 2006: 142; Iijima, 2006: 130–1). However, this idea was not supported by the LDP and Komeito. They were cautious about deployment of aegis destroyers that would be considered as collective self-defense (*Yomiuri Shimbun Seijibu*, 2006: 142–3). The aegis dispatch was not possible until December 2002, when Komeito was finally convinced by the JDA's continuous efforts (*Yomiuri Shimbun Seijibu*, 2006, 143–4).

Two main proposals were finalized to assist US military operations as outlined in the urgent measures of September 19. The first proposal was to send the JMSDF replenishment vessels to the Indian Ocean. The JMSDF thought that refueling operations were feasible because it would be a self-contained effort (*Yomiuri Shimbun Seijibu*, 2006: 140–1). The second proposal was to dispatch the JGSDF troops to Afghanistan to remove landmines. The JGSDF rejected this mission because they insisted that they lacked the skills for such activities (*Yomiuri Shimbun Seijibu*, 2006: 141). As a result, the November 19 assistance measures mainly consisted of maritime activities by the JMSDF: dispatching its two replenishment vessels, three conventional destroyers, two aircraft carriers, and two utility aircrafts of JASDF to the Indian Ocean.

"The Anti-Terrorism Special Measures Law" was passed on October 29, 2001. The JMSDF replenishment vessels and 600 personnel were then deployed in the Indian Ocean and operated to supply oil mainly to the US and British forces. The passage of The Anti-Terrorism Special Measures Law took only 24 days. In terms of consumed hours, it took 62 hours, in comparison with 154 hours for the Law on a Situation in the Areas Surrounding Japan in 1998 and 179 hours for the UNPKO Cooperation Law in 1992. The Koizumi government successfully exercised its leadership in achieving hasty legislation (Shinoda, 2006: 62). Furthermore, in contrast with the Persian Gulf War, legislation was not simply a passive response to US requests but was the outcome of Japan's own ideas and efforts (*Asahi Shimbun*, 2001, October 19: 2).

Did the United States and Japan act as Partners?

The answer is clearly yes. Koizumi's actions were unprecedentedly fast in establishing countermeasure headquarters, summoning the Security Council, announcing the seven anti-terrorist-specific measures on September 19, and promptly legislating with the Anti-Terrorism Special Measures Law on October 29. These speedy behaviors can be understood in the context that Japan had foresight on immediate US attacks on Osama bin Laden and the Taliban in Afghanistan, and Japan had to provide operational assistance to the United States.

The high-profile part of these actions was that Koizumi intentionally avoided constitutional debates. Koizumi was politically aware that constitutional debates would hamper substantial progress in making anti-terrorist measures and legislation. His bypassing strategy in the law-making process represented his strong collective willingness with Bush to fight against terrorists.

Did the United States and Japan have Explicit Collective Interests or a Common Good?

Yes. The prompt actions of the Japanese Government represented its shared interest with the United States against the terrorist attacks. Koizumi's order to Omi to rush to the scene of the terrorist attacks in

New York on September 11, launching the PMOR liaison office within only 45 minutes and Japan's upgrade to the PMOR Countermeasures Headquarters within the next hour, explicitly show Japan's shared interest. JDA Director Nakatani's immediate return from East Timor and his leadership to revise the Self-Defense Law also represented such an identical interest. Japan's announcement of the seven anti-terrorism countermeasures on September 19 and the swift legislation enabling the JMSDF to be engaged in the Indian Ocean explicitly showed Japan's explicit collective security interest against terrorists.

The excessive emphasis of the Koizumi government on speedy behavior was clearly derived from the Japanese Government's trauma during the Persian Gulf War. Nevertheless, this trauma was not just for Tokyo but also for the Japan desk in Washington, such as Hill or Armitage. The US-Japan community of practice recognized promptness as a decisive element in post-September 11 policy-making. The community of practice strongly supported Koizumi's highly intuitive statesmanship on US-Japan political relations.

Did the United States and Japan have Collective Strategic Perspectives?

Yes. Washington was aware that Japan was not able to join combat. Nevertheless, Bush highly regarded Japan's effort in the non-combat area to assist US retaliatory military actions against the Taliban regime in Afghanistan. In contrast with the Persian Gulf War, Japan was confident in immediate US retaliatory attacks on Osama bin Laden, and human participation was inevitably important. The center of the discussion at the Japanese PMOR was how the JSDF overseas dispatch becomes "feasible" within constitutional constrains rather than simply whether the JSDF should be sent or not, in the case of the Persian Gulf War. This sharp difference marked Japan's learning curve on past US behaviors.

The dispatch of the JMSDF replenishment vessels itself can be seen as a deviation in Japan's comprehensive security orientation since 1980. It means that Japan moved slightly away from its security orientation emphasizing foreign aid for nurturing "secured" international environments to traditional military defense (Sakai, 2003: 93). Indeed, after this JMSDF dispatch, the Japanese Government introduced the Military Emergency Law in early December 2001 for Japan's own national security against terrorist attacks by nuclear, biological, and chemical weapons. Japan started studying the Military Emergency Law in 1977, but it had been controversial because it reminded people of the wartime militarism that controlled the entire national life. The September

11 terrorist attacks finally encouraged the passage of the Military Emergency Law.

Did the Shared Collective Strategic Perspectives of the United States and Japan Influence the Process and Outcome of the Deliberations?

Yes. As previously referenced, the upgrade of the PMOR liaison office to its Countermeasures Headquarters was the case. In contrast with the liaison office's function to gather information, the Countermeasures Headquarters was able to assemble concerned ministerial officials and coordinate their activities. The crudest case was perhaps the exclusion of Foreign Minister Tanaka from the decision-making process. She was a hindrance in devising confident and fast policy-making.

Focusing on "prompt" policy-making, Koizumi certainly used the PMOR's enhanced power that was created by institutional reform in the 1990s. A good example was Deputy Chief Cabinet Secretary Furukawa's role of conducting a speedy decision-making process (Hisae, 2002: 8). Nevertheless, more significantly, Koizumi used a "bypass" law-making "method" to make it possible and easy. In the past, the usual law-making process began at the LDP subcommittees; then moved on to approval at the LDP Executive Council, the agreement among the ruling parties that make up the coalition government; cabinet approval; the submission of bills to the Diet; debate with the opposition parties at the Diet; and, finally, the passage of the bills. However, Koizumi chose a reversed path in that he started by obtaining agreement from the coalition partners, Komeito and the Conservative Party, before a consensus was generated within the LDP (Shinoda, 2004: 58). Koizumi was confident that the LDP Diet Members would not oppose the ruling parties' agreement, which would have meant that they were hostile against Koizumi, who was widely supported by the Japanese public (Shinoda, 2004: 58–60).

The Koizumi cabinet brought the new bill to the opposition parties and finally went to the LDP Executive Council to explain the bill's contents. Unsurprisingly, the LDP Diet Members, in particular the influential *zoku giin* (policy tribes),[4] were furious. However, their aggravation was not strong enough to stop the bill (Shinoda, 2004: 59–60). The Special Measures Bill to Fight Terrorism was passed with little revision at the House of Representatives' Special Committee, then passed at the House of Representatives on September 18, and finally passed at the House of Councilors on October 29, 2001.

Finally, Koizumi chose not to enter the debate on "collective self-defense" to make fast agreement from the ruling parties. The Japanese governmental interpretation was that Japan holds the right of collective self-defense according to international law but cannot use it according to Article 9 of its Constitution; therefore, constitutional reinterpretation might be required. Komeito had traditionally been a strong proponent of Article 9. To win consent from Komeito, Koizumi avoided constitutional debates. The Koizumi cabinet characterized the new law, called the Anti-Terrorism Special Measures Law, not as an exertion of collective self-defense with the United States but as a piece of anti-terrorism legislation that was to implement preventive measures against further terrorism in accordance with UN Security Council Resolutions (Shinoda, 2004: 59).

Conclusion

This chapter examined the discourse and behaviors of Japan and the United States in the case of the September 11 terrorist attacks to confirm their collective identity.

In discourse, the Japanese Government in the post-September 11 period frequently used terms such as humankind, democracy, freedom, and peace in contrast to inhuman, barbaric acts and evil in its many official statements. Koizumi's dramatic phrase "I stand by you" at the US-Japan Summit on September 25 represented Japan's strong collective identity with the United States in fighting against bin Laden. The symbolic term also came from Washington. The "show the flag" statement from Hill or Armitage explicitly expressed Washington's desire to gain visible support from Tokyo. This led to the scope of the seven anti-terrorism-specific measures on September 19 clarifying phrases on Japan's prompt and quick "measures" against terrorists to assist the United States. These tones were consistent with the G8 joint statement on September 20, a statement at the Ceremony for All Victims of Terrorist Attacks in the US on September 23, a statement on October 8 when US forces began military strikes in Afghanistan, and a statement on October 29 when the Anti-Terrorism Special Measure Law was passed at the Diet.

Regarding behaviors, four questions were raised. Did the United States and Japan act as partners? Did the United States and Japan have explicit collective interests or common goals? Did the United States and Japan have collective strategic perspectives? Did the shared collective strategic perspectives of the US and Japan influence the process and outcome of the deliberations? All of these questions were answered "yes." These results indicate the high probability of the US-Japan security community.

Notes

1 See page 81–2.
2 This name was changed to "the Anti-terrorism Special Measures Law" to avoid throwing the discussion at the Diet into confusion. See *Asahi Shimbun* (2001, October 5: 2; 2001, October 6: 3).
3 See page 81–2.
4 *Zoku giin* denotes the Diet members who specialize in particular policy areas, such as finance, agriculture, public transportation, health, or defense. These politicians usually maintain their own channels with particular ministries or agencies so that they can intervene in the bill-making process from the very beginning at each ministry. In exchange, the *zoku giin* work to defend the ministries' status quo, and ministries depend on these Diet members to pass bills at the Diet. In this sense, *zoku giin* bureaucrats hold interdependent relationships.

5 Cementing Collective Identity
The Tohoku Earthquake (2011)

Introduction

This chapter will examine the discourse and behaviors that occurred between the United States and Japan from March 11, 2011, when the great earthquake and tsunami hit the northeast coast of Japan and the nuclear disaster occurred at the Fukushima Daiichi Nuclear Power Plant, to May 4, 2011, when the United States Marines finished their humanitarian relief missions and returned to the their home base in Okinawa. In doing so, this chapter will analyze how Japan and the United States interacted with one another in their response to great natural disaster that caused 15,000 deaths.

There are several reasons why this paper will examine the case of the 2011 Tohoku Earthquake. First, it is not about war or terrorism, which can visibly reveal "others." Examples of this include Iraq under the dictatorship of Saddam Hussein during the Persian Gulf War (1990– 1) in Chapter 3, and Osama bin Laden in the case of the September 11 terrorist attacks (2001) in Chapter 4, which can be categorized as others because Japan and the United States collectively perceived that Hussein or bin Laden were violators of humanity, morality, or norms of international society. As argued in Chapter 2, "others" do *not* have to be other states, but they can be the country's own *past*. It can be self-reflexive differentiation practices that treat a past as its reference point (Rumelili, 2007: 27).

Second, this case involved the United States Forces, Japan (USFJ). This case will reveal how US military personnel reacted to the earthquake in terms of a collective identity with the Japanese people. Japan can be assumed to be "the second home country" for the US military personnel who are stationed in Japan. Many of them brought their family and have spent a long time in this country. Therefore, I assume that it was natural for them to take actions to help the Japanese people who lost their family members, homes, or property.

This is not only about the US side, but also that of Japan. This chapter assumes that the ordinary Japanese people's perception of the USFJ drastically changed. The public image of the USFJ has been consistently "bad" since its stationing started in 1945, even though the USFJ had pledged its defense of Japan since the Cold War era. The symbol of this negative image of the USFJ is Okinawa, where 75 percent of all USFJ bases are located. The repeated reports by the Japanese news media on the crimes of US military personnel in Okinawa had consolidated their negative images among the Japanese public for a long time. The Japanese general perception of the USFJ has been that their purpose of being stationed in Japan is to use Japan to deploy their offensive forces toward the Middle East (the Persian Gulf War in 1991) or Southeast Asia (the Vietnam War in 1960s), and not to protect the Japanese people.

Finally, this case involved the "first" joint operations of the JSDF and the USFJ in their alliance history. Their activities were not an exercise but "real" operations that were mobilized to respond to emergencies. This chapter assumes that it was the changes in perception that occurred between the two entities that led to a collective identity through their mutual interactions. In particular, as this paper will address below, the role of the United States Marines in the operation of humanitarian relief missions was critically important.

Puzzles

There are some questions about the 2011 Tohoku Earthquake. Why did the United States provide prompt and large-scale assistance to help Japan, even though there were several bilateral political issues? The 2011 Tohoku Earthquake also caused a nuclear disaster. Many foreign residents in Japan, including Americans, were in a state of panic, and they chartered airplanes to "evacuate" from Japan. The US Government flew the first chartered airplanes carrying 100 US citizens to Taiwan on March 17. The US Government then decided that 600 family members of US diplomats living in Tokyo, Yokohama, and Nagoya were to leave Japan. The US Department of Defense announced that 20,000 family members of USFJ personnel were to leave Japan soon (*Yomiuri Shimbun*, 2011, March 18, Evening Edition: 2). This was the so-called "Operation Pacific Passage." Operation Pacific Passage showed enormous US fear of being exposed to radioactive material from the Fukushima Daiichi Nuclear Power Station.

Furthermore, the US Government did not trust the official information that was provided by the Japanese Government on the nuclear disaster. This accelerated US fear (*Asahi Shimbun*, 2001, March 18: 5). It is natural for the United States not to become involved in any activities that would endanger US citizens. Nevertheless, the US Government not only sent its special units that address nuclear incidents to assist the Japanese Government, but also decided to execute a major operation to rescue Japanese people—despite the danger of being exposed to radiation.

How can I explain these US behaviors? They could be explained by classical realism. As George F. Kennan said during the Cold War, because Japan is one of the five major industrial areas in the world, the United States needs to secure it as its ally against opponents (Kennan, 1947). Kennan aimed at the rapid rehabilitation of the Japanese economy in the postwar period so that it would become an important member of the US grand alliance against the Soviet Union. This scheme affected the occupation policy of the Supreme Commander of Allied Powers (SCAP) to re-industrialize Japan to become a fortress against communist threats in Asia. His argument could be applicable to the incidents of 2011. After March 11, 2011, the US Marine Corps took the navigation course from South to North in the Sea of Japan to send an implicit message to neighboring countries that the United States would not allow any country to threaten Japan in such a crisis (Eldridge, 2017: 73).

Nevertheless, this possible explanation would not be sufficient. In contrast to the immediate postwar period in the 1940s, by 2011, Japan had become one of the largest economies in the world. Japan was able to afford its own economic rehabilitation without foreign assistance. Indeed, US assistance was merely humanitarian relief rather than economic aid.

Liberalism could account for these US actions. While realism treats alliances as an expedient against common enemies, liberalism considers alliances as a type of "international organization" that fosters bonds among allies. Alliances themselves can be entities that are somewhat independent from member states in international politics. Haas and Whiting noted that today's alliances have transformed from the calculated alliance of sovereign states into a regional association of peoples united by loyalty to common myths and symbols in addition to concrete interests (Haas and Whiting, 1956: 183). This transformation was a product of the twentieth century in that economic welfare and development demanded coordination with military planning because allocations of human resources and finances are limited (Haas and Whiting, 1956: 183). This argument suggests that today's alliance is an "institution" with its own life. It is not necessary to presuppose that all of the behaviors of the alliance are about balancing against a potential enemy. Rather, it is about the self-preservation of the alliance itself. A highly institutionalized alliance is supposed to quickly respond to any emergencies. The alliance is now transformed into a "security management institution," acquiring various purposes (Keohane and Wallander, 1999).

However, these possible arguments are weak. In the United States–Japan Mutual Security Treaty of 1960, there was no clause on the duties of the USFJ to assist Japan in the case of a natural disaster. The US activities were *not* a result of an institutional mechanism. As Eldridge, who served as part of Operation Tomodachi for the March 11 Earthquake, confessed, there was no preexisting institutional arrangement between the USFJ and JSDF for emergencies. As is argued in detail below, the USFJ was frustratingly waiting for concrete requests and guidance from the Japanese Government for several days even though the USFJ was ready to take action at any time (Eldridge, 2017: 72). The Japanese Government and even the JSDF did not have much knowledge on the capability and equipment that were possessed by the USFJ (Eldridge, 2017: 80–3).

Japan

Why did Japan accept US assistance? This question might seem strange because any country needs help in an emergency. Nevertheless, it is a plausible question because the relations between the Japanese people and the USFJ had *not* been "friendly" since 1945, when US forces were first stationed in Japan. In particular, March 11 was "bad timing." Immediately before the Earthquake, the Japanese public was in a state of rage against the discriminative statement that "Okinawa people are masters of extortion," which was made by Kevin Maher, a former US Consul in Okinawa and Chief of the Japan Division of the Bureau of East Asian and Pacific Affairs of the US Department of State.[1] Regardless of whether his words were true, the Japanese public's anger did not diminish (*Asahi Shimbun*, 2011, March 11, 2011: 1, 3; *Asahi Shimbun*, 2011, Evening Edition, March 11: 14). Maher resigned three days after the news media's reports appeared (*Asahi Shimbun*, 2011, March 11: 3), but he changed his mind and stayed in office because he wanted to utilize his rich knowledge of the USFJ and nuclear power plants in Japan to help with the post-earthquake humanitarian assistance (*Asahi Shimbun*, 2011, March 16, Evening Edition: 2).

The Maher issue was rooted in many years of the Futenma Air Base issue. The return of Futenma Air Base to the local owners was a long-cherished desire for the people of Okinawa; therefore, Japan and the

United States negotiated its feasibility. Maher's words complicated this issue. Against such a political backdrop, it is surprising that Japan accepted the large scale of US humanitarian relief.

There was a precedent for Japan to reject the USFJ's disaster relief. It was the case of the 1995 Hanshin Awaji Earthquake when Tomiichi Murayama, the president of the Japan Socialist Party (JSP), was prime minister. The JSP historically had not recognized the JSDF and the US-Japan Security Treaty as being constitutional. The JSP maintained unarmed neutrality as a party platform and therefore did not recognize the USFJ as a legitimate force in Japan. It was logical for Murayam not to accept the USFJ's assistance—even for disaster relief.

Changes in domestic politics might explain why Japan welcomed US assistance for the March 11 earthquake. Prime Minister Kan was the president of the Democratic Party of Japan (DPJ), which recognizes the JSDF and the alliance with the United States as constitutional and a necessary means to defend Japan. Nevertheless, governmental change does not necessitate changes in the Japanese public's emotions against the USFJ. The prolonged base issues and their related problems, including the Maher issue, had never vanished.

The March 11 Tohoku Earthquake

In the afternoon on March 1, 2011, a huge earthquake with a 9.0 magnitude and a tsunami hit the northeast coast of Japan. It destroyed seaports, villages, towns, houses, buildings, railroads, roads, and public infrastructure. This led to a meltdown and the release of radioactive material at the Fukushima Daiichi Nuclear Power Station, which is recognized by international standards as one of the worst nuclear incidents in history, equal to the Chernobyl disaster in Russia 1986. The event caused more than 15,000 deaths, and it left 2,500 missing and 6,000 injured.

Discourse

Immediately after the earthquake occurred on March 11, US President Barack Obama stated:

> This is a potentially catastrophic disaster and the images of destruction of flooding coming out of Japan are simply heartbreaking. Japan is, of course, one of our strongest and closest allies, and this morning I spoke with Prime Minister Kan. On behalf of the American people, I conveyed our deepest condolences, especially

to the victims and their families, and I offered our Japanese friends whatever assistance is needed. We currently have an air craft carrier in Japan, and another is on its way. We also have a ship en route to the Marianas Islands to assist as needed ... Our hearts go out to our friends in Japan and across the region and we're going to stand with them as they recover and rebuild.

(White House, 2011)

US Secretary of State Hillary Clinton offered "immediate disaster relief assistance" (*International Business Times*, 2011, March 12). US Secretary of Defense Robert Gates said, "We will respond to any need" (*Yomiuri Shimbun*, 2011, March 13: 9). The Seventh Fleet announced that two US destroyers, the *USS McCampbell* and *USS Curtis Wilbur* that were stationed off Boso Peninsula, were preparing "to assist Japanese authorities with providing at-sea search and rescue and recovery operations" (*International Business Times*, 2011, March 12). The III Marine Expeditionary Force said that it was "prepositioning forces and supplies in support of humanitarian assistance and disaster relief operations" (*International Business Times*, 2011, March 12). Three days later, while preparing the operations of these military forces, President Obama said, "We will stand with the people of Japan in the difficult days ahead" (*Jiji Press Ticker Service*, 2011, March 15).

Here is where the new vocabulary emerged. Paul Wilcox, who was a retired airman working at the Division of Northeast Asia of the United States Pacific Command (USPACOM), named the efforts "Operation Tomodachi," and USPACOM Commander Robert Willard officially adopted it (*Yomiuri Shimbun*, 2011, May 20: 4). "Tomodachi" means "friend" in Japanese. Wilcox told the Japanese news media that he wanted to inform the Japanese people that the United States would behave in accordance with a proverb, "A friend in need is a friend indeed" (*Yomiuri Shimbun*, 2011, May 20: 4). The word "friend" frequently appeared in various phases of US activities. Andrew MacMannis, Commander of the 31st Marine Expeditionary Unit (31MEU), publically stated on the way to Japan from Malaysia that he prayed for the Japanese people, who are "our good friends and allies" (Eldridge, 2017: 63). Adrian Ragland, the Captain of the USS Tortuga, a dock landing ship, said that this was a good opportunity to demonstrate the strength of the US-Japan relationship (*Yomiuri Shimbun*, 2011, March 15, 2011: 4). George Aguilar, the commander of the HS-4 Black Knights, a helicopter squadron on the *Ronald Reagan*, an aircraft carrier, said, "What we are doing here is diplomacy. This is our best friend in the region" (*International Herald Tribune*, 2011, March 23: 2). Captain David Fluker of an amphibious assault vessel said "What we are here for is to stop the pain and stop the suffering and ensure that life gets back to normal as soon as possible for our friends in Japan" (*New York Times*, 2011, March 23: 13). US Ambassador to Japan John Roos visited Ishinomaki city, the quake-hit area, to console victims on March 23, and he said, "The United States will support our Japanese friend with anything" (*Yomiuri Shimbun*, 2011, March 24: 12). Paul Feather, colonel of the 374 Airlift Wing Commander, stated in a public interview at the Yokota Airbase, "Japan, where I now live, is almost my home. There are many Japanese working here at this base, and I want to do anything to support them" (*Yomiuri Shimbun*, 2011, March 30: 25; Japan Economic Newswire, 2011, March 29). Captain Thom W. Burke, Commanding Officer of the *USS Ronald Reagan*, said, "All the crew members are proud of helping Japan" (*Asahi Shimbun*, 2011, March 23: 5). The Commander of the US Pacific Fleet, Patrick Walsh, who directed Operation Tomodachi, said, "We rush to the scene of Japan's crisis without expecting any reward. It is a proof of real friendship … Operation Tomodachi is a symbol of friendship and close cooperation between the Japanese and the American people" (*Yomiuri Shimbun*, 2011, April 9: 2, 4). State Secretary Clinton said in April, "We responded to this crisis as a friend, not just as an ally" (*Asahi Shimbun*, 2011, April 18: 14).

Japan also expressed its sense of friendship in its public statement. Japanese Defense Minister Toshimi Kitazawa visited the USS aircraft carrier *Ronald Reagan* on April 4, and said, "We appreciate the Army, Navy, Air Force and Marines of the United States for their unusual scale of assistance operations. This is a sign of our bond" (*Asahi Shimbun*, 2011, April 7: 3). He also said, "I have never been more encouraged by and proud of the fact that the United States is our ally" (*Asahi Shimbun*, 2011, April 5: 4). Masanori Ide, the captain of the Japan Land SDF and a liaison officer with the 76 mission corps of the US Navy, said in an interview that, "I saw that the marines and seamen were devoted to rescue missions not because they were ordered to do so but because they wanted to do something for their friends" (Eldridge, 2017: 118). Japanese Foreign Minister Takeaki Matsumto spoke at a press conference and stated that the Japan–United States partnership in disaster relief activities has "greatly encouraged Japan" (*BBC Monitoring Asia Pacific*, 2011, April 15).

As the Operation entered the terminal phase in April, Kenneth Gluck, the Okinawa Area Coordinator (OAC) said, "The Japan-United States bond has been strengthened under this difficult situation." Hidetoshi Hirata, a liaison officer in Okinawa, said, "Japan and the United States acted together without any plan and produced a good result. It was very meaningful to build confidence between us" (*Asahi Shimbun*, 2011, April 16: 27).

Prime Minister Naoto Kan formally stated

> Immediately after the earthquake, the United States, our most important friend and ally, provided swift cooperation. President Obama kindly called me to convey his strong commitment that the United States stood ready to provide all-out support to the Japanese people during this time of great difficulty. He reaffirmed that the relationship between our nations is unshakable. So many Japanese citizens, including myself, were enormously encouraged by these remarks.
>
> (Prime Minister of Japan and His Cabinet, 2011, April 15; *The Washington Post*, 2011, April 17: A21)

The USFJ also invented a term, "Seoul Train," for the activities to remove debris at Nobiru Station of the Sendai Line, Higashi Matsushima City, Miyagi Prefecture. The Sendai Line in the coastal area suffered extensive damage from the earthquake and tsunami. The USFJ and JSDF worked together to restore the line. Captain Alan Nayland, who directed this activity, said, "We want to show the soul of Japanese and Americans in the Sendai Line's restoration" (*Yomiuri Shimbun*, 2011, April 21, Evening Edition: 11; *Asahi Shimbun*, 2011, April 22, Evening Edition: 19).

Behaviors

Immediately after the earthquake occurred on March 11, US Ambassador to Japan Roos made a wake-up call to President Obama to inform him of the disaster. Roos, who experienced the Loma Prieta Earthquake that hit northern California in 1989, sensed that the March 11 earthquake would be more dangerous than the 1989 one (*Yomiuri Shimbun*, 2011, April 13: 4). At 0:15 AM, March 12, Obama and Kan agreed by phone that the United States would provide all-out support, which was later referred to as "Operation Tomodachi" (*Yomiuri Shimbun*, 2011, April 13: 4). At 9:00 AM, USPACOM Commander Willard phoned JSDF Chief of Joint Staff Council Ryoichi Oriki. Willard volunteered for rescue operations, and the Commander of the USFJ Field also announced the immediate commitment of the marines to the affected areas (*Yomiuri Shimbun*, 2011, April 13: 4).

The USFJ had already initiated its own headquarters for disaster control ten minutes after the earthquake occurred and started planning (Eldridge, 2017: 37). The 31st Marine Expeditionary Unit (31 MEU) now assumed the main role because it had quality equipment. For example, the amphibious assault ship *USS Essex* is capable of mounting 30 helicopters, which can execute search-and-rescue missions, deliver shipments, and provide medical treatment at its on-ship hospital. Nevertheless, when the Earthquake occurred, *Essex* was stopped at a port in Malaysia after a joint naval exercise in Cambodia. *USS Harpers Ferry*, a dock landing ship, was sailing toward Indonesia to participate in the multilateral disaster drill of the ASEN Regional Forum (ARF). *USS Germantown*, another dock landing ship, was deployed in another location in Indonesia (Eldridge, 2017: 62). Despite these deployments, *Essex* left Malaysia for Japan within 24 hours of receiving an emergency phone call from the 7th Fleet (Eldridge, 2017: 24). *Harpers Ferry* and *Germantown* approached near the port of Indonesia; however, they quickly changed their routes toward Japan. The marines on board *Harpers Ferry* were on high alert as they monitored the situation developing in Japan; when they learned that they would sail to Japan to serve in rescue missions, there was an outpouring of joy (Eldridge, 2017: 63). The *USS Ronald Reagan* was sailing toward South Korea to join the joint exercise but changed its course and arrived off Sanriku in the morning of March 13, and it began its co-operation with the JSDF (*Asahi Shimbun*, 2011, March 14: 4; *Asahi Shimbun*, 2011, March 23: 5; *Yomiuri Shimbun*, 2011, March 15: 6). The *Ronald Reagan* prepared to serve as a floating platform for refueling aircrafts of the JASDF and the USFJ for their rescue and recovery activities ashore (*International Business Times*, 2011, March 12). The flagship of the 7th Fleet, *USS Blue Ridge* in Singapore, set its course to Japan.

Operation Tomodachi also involved control of the Fukushima Daiichi Nuclear Power Station, which caused the second "disaster." The United States paid enormous attention to this disaster. Japan and the United States recognized the spread of radioactive material as a common threat. The United States Nuclear Regulatory Commission (USNRC) dispatched its two specialists to Japan on March 12 (*Yomiuri Shimbun*, 2011, March 14: 9). The US Department of Defense sent nine specialists who would organize a team to evaluate the damage management. USPACOM Commander Willard prepared to gather a team of 450 nuclear specialists and was willing to support any activities on the nuclear disaster from surveillance to decontamination (*Yomiuri Shimbun*, 2011, March 18, Evening Edition: 2; *Asahi Shimbun*, 2011, March 18, Evening Edition: 3). The United States put pressure on Japan to cool down the nuclear reactor by dropping seawater on it (*Yomiuri Shimbun*, 2011, March 18, Evening Edition: 2). The United States also flew an unmanned aerial vehicle, *Global Hawk*, and an ultra-high altitude reconnaissance U2 aircraft to monitor the status of the damaged power plants. The US Marine Corps sent 140 marines from the Chemical Biological Incident Response Force (CBIRF), which can counter the effects of chemical, biological, radiological, nuclear, or high-yield explosive (CBRNE) incidents (*Asahi Shimbun*, 2011, April 1: 2). The CBIRF publically demonstrated its capabilities and skills at a joint drill on nuclear contamination with the JSDF at the US Yokota Air Base (*Yomiuri Shimbun*, 2011, April 9, Evening Edition: 2; *Asahi Shimbun*, 2011, April 10: 4). The US Air Force dispatched the Air Force Radiation Assessment Team (AFRAT). AFRAT members performed radiological assessments at Sendai Airport on April 5, 2011 (United States Air Force, 2011, April 5). The US Army sent the 9th Area Medical Laboratory (AML) to Japan. The 9th AML can perform surveillance, confirmatory analytical lab testing, and health hazard assessments of environmental, occupational, endemic, and chemical, biological, radiological, nuclear, and explosive threats (United States Army, 2011, April 14). AML checked for radioactive material contained in the air in Japan (*Yomiuri Shimbun*, 2011, April 15, Evening Edition: 2).

In contrast to the 1995 Great Hanshin Earthquake, the Japanese Government formally requested disaster relief from the US Government on the night of March 11 (*Asahi Shimbun*, 2011, March 12: 17). Immediately, the USPACOM officially announced Operation Tomodachi. According to Robert Eldridge—the Deputy Assistant Chief of Staff, Government and External Affairs (G7), Marine Corps Installations Pacific/Marine Forces Japan—because the Japanese Government had promptly accepted US assistance, the co-operation of disaster relief between Japan and the United States in the March 11 earthquake was much faster than in the case of the 1995 earthquake.[2] Indeed, the USFJ and JSDF worked closely together from March 11.

In the morning of March 12, an investigation team that consisted of four USFJ officers, including Eldridge, and two JSDF officers investigated the Sendai Airport, which had been rendered useless by the tsunami. Eldridge advised the immediate restoration of the Sendai Airport to transport a vast amount of goods to be supplied to the affected areas (Eldridge, 2017: 38). Collaborative efforts day and night by staff members of Sendai Airport, local business workers, the JASDF, the US Marines, and the US Air Force restored the function of the eastern half of a runway, and the first flight of a C-130 transport aircraft arrived there on March 16 (Eldridge, 2017: 39; *Asahi Shimbun*, 2011, March 18: 30). Through the efforts of the 353rd Special Operations Group of the US Air Force, Sendai Airport resumed its civilian operations one month later (*New York Times*, 2011, April 14: 6). At the same time, the

JASDF and 31MEU started using Yamagata Airport to load equipment needed to establish a forward-refueling base there (Eldridge, 2017: 39). Yamagata Airport then became the main base, operational within 24 hours for the disaster relief operations of both JSDF and the USFJ (*Asahi Shimbun*, 2011, March 21: 14).

The *USS Tortuga*, a dock landing ship that carried 273 soldiers of the 5th Brigade of the Japan Ground Self-Defense Force (JGSDF) with a total of 93 vehicles, such as trucks and wreckers, landed at Mutsu City facing the Ōminato Bay. This was the "first" transfer of the Japan SDF by a US ship ever in the JSDF's history (*Asahi Shimbun*, 2011, March 18: 14; *Asahi Shimbun*, 2011, March 23: 5).

The United States created the Joint Support Force (JSF) at the Yokota Air Base in Japan for the first time in its history. For the United States, the JSF is identical to the Joint Task Force (JTF) in wartime. The JSF or JTF functions as "the general headquarters" of the front line, which unifies the army, navy, air force, and marines. This represented US recognition of the March 11 earthquake as being equivalent to a war (*Asahi Shimbun*, 2011, April 7: 3). Commander of the USFJ Burton Field was initially the JSF Commander; however, he was soon replaced by a higher-ranking officer, Commander of the US Pacific Fleet Patrick Walsh (*Yomiuri Shimbun*, 2011, March 28: 2; *Asahi Shimbun*, 2011, April 7: 3).

Japan created its own JTF in Sendai that was directed by Lieutenant General Eiji Kimizuka. In accordance with the Guidelines of US-Japan Defense Cooperation in 1997 (Japanese Ministry of Defense, 2011: 18; *Yomiuri Shimbun*, 2011, April 13: 4), Japan created a Bilateral Crisis Action Team (BCAT) office by dispatching a liaison team of ten officers headed by Defense Division Chief, Ground Staff Office (GSO), JGSDF Koichiro Bansho to the JSF. It was rare for Japanese high-ranking defense officers to be stationed at a US military base (*Asahi Shimbun*, 2011, April 7: 3). Japan also established BCAT offices within the JTF, Sendai, and the Ministry of Defense in Tokyo to enhance their linkage with the USFJ (Eldridge, 2016: 27). Thom Burke later said that the BCAT smoothed US-Japan collaborative activities (*Yomiuri Shimbun*, 2011, April 21: 2).

The JSDF and the USFJ worked together in search and rescue operations immediately after March 11. Nevertheless, there were still 18,000 people missing at the end of March. From April 1 to 3, 18,000 members of the JSDF, 7,000 members of the USFJ, the Japan Coast Guard, police forces, and fire departments, executed search operations in the coastal areas of Iwate, Miyagi, and Fukushima prefectures. Japan and the United States mobilized 130 aircrafts and 90 ships for this three-day operation. They found 79 dead bodies during this three-day intensive search (*Asahi Shimbun*, 2011, April 1: 2; *Asahi Shimbun*, 2011, April 2: 30; *Yomiuri Shimbun*, 2011, April 2, Evening Edition: 1; *Yomiuri Shimbun*, 2011, April 4, Evening Edition: 11).

The control of the nuclear reactors at Fukushima Station was another common task for Japan and the United States. However, there was a gap in the sense of crisis between the United States and Japan. The United States nuclear power stations had stockpiled cooling devices since the September 11 terrorist attacks. The US Air Force had been ready to carry this equipment to anywhere in the United States. US Secretary of State Hillary Clinton ordered that this equipment be sent to Japan; however, the Japanese Government refused to use it because it thought there was plenty of nearby seawater (*Yomiuri Shimbun*, 2011, April 1: 2). Japan indeed used seawater; however, the US Government strongly urged Japan to stop because the sea salt would corrode the nuclear reactors (*Asahi Shimbun*, 2011, March 26: 5). Ultimately, Japan borrowed a barge from the USFJ that carried a pump that could hold 1,000 tons of fresh water to be used to cool down the reactor (*Yomiuri Shimbun*, 2011, April 1: 5, 31). This issue generated emotional friction between the US and Japanese governments. According to former nuclear scientist Jun Sakurai, the United States has a high capability for risk management, while Japan has no plan to manage a nuclear crisis (*Asahi Shimbun*, 2011, May 22: 1). On March 16, the White House decided to move forward with its own measures rather than wait for the Japanese Government's requests. The US Government became skeptical of Japan's capability to respond to a nuclear disaster (*Asahi Shimbun*, 2011, April 7: 3). On March 17, President Obama showed Prime Minister Kan a list of items for radioactive management and decontamination, which the United States could promptly provide to Japan (*Asahi Shimbun*, 2011, May 22: 3).

These deficiencies in Japan's recognition, knowledge, skills, and equipment in the joint operations were reflected throughout the entire process of the operations. The 31 MEU could have moved a week earlier if a prior consultation system between the JSDF and the USFJ had been established (Eldridge, 2016: 30). As noted above, the JSDF and the USFJ never knew what they had that could be mutually deployed. Further, as noted above, a US military ship had never loaded JSDF vehicles; for example, the *USS Tortuga* carried JGSDF vehicles in Ominato Bay. It was the first time that a US Navy aircraft carrier provided a platform for air operations of JASDF helicopters. Even within the BCAT in Sendai, there were often conversations between the

JSDF and the USFJ; for example, the USFJ would ask, "What do you need?" and the JSDF would reply, "What do you have?" It was as if the JSDF and the USFJ had never met before (Eldridge, 2016: 29).

Andrew MacMannis, colonel of the 31st Marine Expeditionary Corp, later confessed that both the JGSDF and JMSDF knew nothing about the US Marine Corps. The JGSDF simply recognized the US Marines as a naval force, whereas the JMSDF saw it as a ground force; therefore, both of them did not believe that it was necessary to work with the US Marines (Eldridge, 2016: 47–8). Their lack of recognition delayed the bilateral co-planning of disaster relief. In this sense, Operation Tomodachi was the beginning of US-Japan security institutionalization (Imai, 2012: 66). Nevertheless, this would be a useful experience for future policy on disaster relief. Coastal communities in Aichi, Mie, Kochi, and Hyogo prefectures showed an interest in learning about Operation Tomodachi (*The Japan Times*, 2012, March 3: 1).

Did the United States and Japan Behave as Partners?

The answer is yes. There are many instances of this. At both civilian and military levels, the United States acted promptly to assist Japan. The swift communication of US Ambassador Roos with President Obama after the earthquake led to the telephone conference between Obama and Kan. The USFJ established its own headquarters for disaster control ten minutes after the earthquake hit Japan. Although the major ships of the 31MEU—*Essex*, *Germantown*, and *Harpers Ferry*—were deployed in Southeast Asia, they eagerly rushed to Japan. 31MEU Commander MacMannis later said that he began mapping out the disaster relief plan before the 7th Fleet formally ordered him to return to Japan. Essex took six days to reach Japan; thus, crews used their time to develop the operation plan (Eldridge, 2016: 43–6).

Japan also acted as a partner. In contrast to the 1995 Hanshin Awaji Earthquake, Japan accepted US willingness to assist in disaster relief immediately after the earthquake occurred. This enabled the JSDF to work closely with the USFJ. The establishment of the BCAT in Sendai, Tokyo, and Yokota represented Japan's collective agreement with the United States to counter the effects of one of the worst natural disasters that Japan had ever experienced. Although there were institutional flaws that impeded the ability of the JSDF and the USFJ to cope with the natural disaster together, Japan showed a willingness to overcome this and maximize the power of bilateral collaborative actions. From these behaviors, I judged the past rejection of disaster relief mission of USFJ in 1995 as others.

Did the United States and Japan have Explicit Collective Interests or a Common Good?

The answer is positive. Both Japan and the United States engaged in the search for survivors and the restoration of public infrastructure such as roads, railroads, seaports, airports, electricity, and other lifelines. Japan and the United States shared an awareness of the dangers of the radioactive material from the Fukushima Daiichi Nuclear Power Station. The US Marines sent the CBIRF to Japan and instructed the JSDF on how to counter radioactive exposure. Although there was a gap in their threat recognition on measures that addressed explosions in nuclear plants, Japan and the United States nevertheless worked together.

Did the United States and Japan have Collective Strategic Perspectives?

The answer is yes. Japan was aware that this crisis needed to be overcome as soon as possible. The loss of 2.5 billion Yen and the unemployment of 120,000 Japanese citizens that resulted from the disaster was perhaps Japan's greatest national challenge after World War II. For the United States, the restoration of Japan was also critically important for both economic and geopolitical reasons. US Secretary of State Clinton visited Tokyo on April 16 to promise continuous US support for Japanese private sectors. Thomas Donohue, president of the US Chamber of Commerce, accompanied Clinton in talks with the Japanese Business Federation for this purpose (*BBC Monitoring Asia Pacific*, 2011, April 17). The United States was also cautious about the possibility that North Korea or China might exploit this crisis politically. The route from Southeast Asia to the Sea of Japan, which the 31MEU took in March, was a tacit US message to China and North Korea that the United States would not allow them to touch devastated Japan (Eldridge, 2017: 73).

Did the Shared Collective Strategic Perspectives of the United States and Japan Influence the Process and Outcome of the Deliberations?

This case study revealed that Japan's disaster relief operations required a close relationship with the United States. Before the March 11 Tohoku Earthquake, Japanese experts on natural disasters, the Japanese Government, and the JSDF had never considered the USFJ to be Japan's partner with manpower, rich experience, skills, knowledge on disaster relief, and equipment. Rather, Japan had recognized the USFJ as "a foreign aid organization" (Eldridge, 2016: 2–8). However, this perception changed, and the change is reflected in a US-Japan joint statement dated June 21, 2011 that their bilateral cooperation for Operation Tomodachi became a model for future disaster relief operations, such as making the BCAT, countermeasures for nuclear accidents, and intimate relationships between the local communities and the USFJ (Japanese Ministry of Foreign Affairs, 2011). This national level of recognition also spread to local communities such as Shizuoka, Kochi, Wakayama, and Mie that have an interest in disaster prevention with the United States (Eldridge, 2016: 9–10).

Conclusion

This chapter examined the case of the March 11 Tohoku Earthquake to confirm the US-Japan collective identity, which is an essential part of their bilateral security community, and scrutinized the discourse and behaviors during disaster relief, the so-called Operation Tomodachi. The results are as follows.

In the discourse analysis, I found the development of a new vocabulary of "friendship." The name of the operation itself was "tomodachi," which means "friend" in Japanese. The "friend" phrase was found elsewhere among US political leaders, marines, sailors, airmen, and soldiers. This was also true on the Japanese side. Japan gradually recognized US behaviors as an expression of "friendship" rather than simply the expression of an ally.

In the behavioral analysis, this paper raised four questions. Did the United States and Japan act as partners? Did the United States and Japan have explicit collective interests or common goals? Did the United States and Japan have collective strategic perspectives? Did the shared collective strategic perspectives of the US and Japan influence the process and outcome of the deliberations? The answer to these four questions is yes. This confirmation informs us of the high possibility of a security community between Japan and the United States.

Notes

1 Maher himself contended that he never said such insulting words against the Okinawa people. See *Wall Street Journal* http://realtime.wsj.com/japan/2011/04/14/.
2 Robert D. Eldridge was the political adviser to the forward-deployed command of US forces during Operation Tomodachi. He was a graduate student at Kobe University when the 1995 Hanshin Awaji Earthquake occurred. He was convinced, according to his personal experience, that the March 11 Earthquake proved the significance of close cooperation of the USFJ and JSDF for disaster relief to save victims and in the recovery of the affected area. See Eldridge (2016: 37).

6 Conclusion
New Understanding on the US-Japan Relationship

Introduction

This study aimed to show that the US-Japan relationship is that of a security community. This study considers the "we-feeling" or collective identity as the most important element of the relationship. To show this, three case studies were conducted on the Persian Gulf War (1990–1), the September 11 terrorist attacks (2001), and the March 11 Tohoku Earthquake (2011). To this end, I employed Cronin's two-path approach.

The first path examined the nature of discourse among specific political actors, in particular, within the US-Japan community of practice. The most certain sign that a new concept or understanding has been adopted is *the development of new vocabulary* that is publicly articulated (Cronin, 1999: 15). Specifically, this is required to judge whether the community of practice speaks of a special bond among the members.

The second path analyzed the behaviors of the actors. We need to determine whether the specified actors behave in a manner consistent with their identities in circumstances in which they would otherwise not be expected to do so. Following Cronin's method (Cronin, 1999: 16–17), this study asked four questions in each case. First, *Did the United States and Japan act as partners?* Second, *Did the United States and Japan have explicit collective interests or a common good?* Third, *Did the United States and Japan have collective strategic perspectives?* Finally, *Did the shared collective strategic perspectives of the United States and Japan influence the process and outcome of the deliberations?* Each case study had its own answers to these questions.

A Summary of Results

Discourse

In the case of the Persian Gulf War, the United States and Japan recognized Saddam Hussein as the "other." President Bush and Prime

Minister Kaifu both spoke of Hussein as a violator of international law and norms. Nevertheless, a discrepancy between their discourses soon emerged, revealing that their interests were not entirely compatible. While the United States expected Japan to play a tangible role in the US-led multinational coalition against Hussein, Japan was not aware of the importance of this in the beginning of the crisis. Nevertheless, Japan soon learned of the need for "human participation" in the multinational coalition that could be within its constitutional constrains. In the course of the discourse, Japan's understanding of anti-Hussein measures was anchored in the United Nations rather than in its alliance with the United States. For the United States, the national interest represented by Bush's remark of a "new world order" is synonymous to the UN-based order. His references to "solidarity," "international community," "common decision," "common interests," and "collective efforts" revealed such a US notion.

These differences also appeared in the discourse expressing their approaches to the event, with terms such as "responsibility" and "vision" from the United States and "contribution" (kōken) from Japan. As a result, this study found a great negativity on the US side concerning such a discrepancy. There was *no* development of new vocabulary within the US-Japan community of practice.

In the case of the September 11 terrorist attacks, this discrepancy disappeared. President Bush welcomed Prime Minister Koizumi's frequent references to "prompt" and "dispatching the Self-Defense Forces." Koizumi's dichotomy between "freedom, peace and democracy," and "terrorism, barbaric acts and inhumanity" also well matched the US notion of the "War on Terror." Campbell was correct in his judgment that the solidarity represented at the US-Japan summit on September 25 was a breakthrough for US-Japan relations.

The most striking part of their discourse was the term "show the flag." Armitage aimed to create a situation similar to the case of the Persian Gulf War—when Japan was severely criticized as being an automatic teller machine. Hence, Koizumi's conscious use of the words "promptly take necessary measures" only six days after the terrorist attacks was perhaps satisfactory to Armitage and the community of practice. Nevertheless, the phrase "show the flag" connotes a mixture of pressure and expectation.

In the case of the March 11 Tohoku Earthquake, there was finally development of the vocabulary "Operation Tomodachi." The phrase stems from the proverb "a friend in need is a friend indeed." Koizumi used the same expression on September 23, 2001. The term "friend" frequently appeared elsewhere in this case. President Obama said on March 12, "We will stand with the people of Japan in the difficult days ahead." This phrase also resonates with Koizumi's statement "I stand by you" at the US-Japan summit on September 25, 2001. Furthermore, the USFJ created the term "the soul train" for the USFJ-JSDF joint activities to restore the Sendai Line of the railroad.

Behaviors

Let us turn to the nature of the behaviors of the United States and Japan in the three cases: the Persian Gulf War, the September 11 terrorist attacks, and the March 11 Tohoku Earthquake. As Figure 1 shows, this study applied four questions to each case study: (1) Did the United States and Japan act as partners? (2) Did the United States and Japan have explicit collective interests or a common good? (3) Did the United States and Japan have collective strategic perspectives? (4) Did the shared collective strategic perspectives of the United States and Japan influence the process and outcome of the deliberations? The answers to these questions are summarized as follows.

Did the United States and Japan Act as Partners?

All cases answered yes. In the case of the Persian Gulf War, despite many constraints, the United States and Japan made common efforts to materialize the symbolic act of sending the JSDF to the Persian Gulf. Although US effort was seen as "pressure" by the Japanese Government and public and despite the failure of the UNPC bill passage, Prime Minister Kaifu still sought the JSDF dispatch even after the war was over. The sending of the minesweepers to the region in April 1991 was strong evidence for Japan's partnership.

In the case of September 11, Koizumi's behaviors were prompt in establishing countermeasure headquarters, summoning the Security Council, announcing the seven specific anti-terrorist measures on September 19, and promptly passing the Anti-Terrorism Special Measures Law on October 29. These speedy behaviors can be understood in context, considering that Japan had certain expectations that the US would immediately attack the Taliban regime that was protecting bin Laden in Afghanistan and that Japan now ought to assist the US force militarily.

In the case of the March 11 Tohoku Earthquake, the prompt action taken by the United States immediately after the earthquake is strong evidence. In particular, the swift move of the USFJ to aid in disaster relief was a noteworthy event. The establishment of its own headquarters for disaster control only ten minutes after the earthquake and the return of all the major ships of 31MEU from Southeast Asia to Japan was perhaps the most striking act. For Japan, the evidence was its acceptance of such immediate USFJ actions. This led to JSDF-USFJ joint disaster relief operations for the first time ever and the overcoming of many institutional obstacles for the arrangements.

Did the United States and Japan have Explicit Collective Interests or a Common Good?

All cases answered positively. This question is related to what motivated the states to take action. This question resonates with Wendt's discussion on "international states" and their transnational interests (Wendt, 1994). In the Persian Gulf War, the answer was yes because Japan and the United States demanded that Iraq immediately withdraw its occupying force in Kuwait. The US's quick deployment of its forces in Saudi Arabia and Japan's prompt freezing of Kuwait's assets to prevent them from being stolen by Iraq and its financial support of the US forces were explicit evidence.

In the case of September 11, the evidence is Japan's "prompt" actions. To overcome the trauma of the Persian Gulf War, Japan's anti-terrorist measures and legislation were perhaps unprecedentedly fast in the history of Japan's foreign policy. The US-Japan community of practice played the central role in supporting the Koizumi government's political maneuver to pass this legislation.

In the case of the March 11 earthquake, it was clear that Japan and the United States collectively engaged in activities for disaster relief and humanitarian assistance in various areas, including dealing with the danger of radioactive materials from the nuclear power station.

Did the United States and Japan have Collective Strategic Perspectives?

For the Persian Gulf War, the answer was mixed. Japan had a limited understanding of the US tactics against Iraqi forces. Japan was not able to respond to the US request for concrete equipment for military operations. Nevertheless, at a strategic level, Japan was aware that US forces would eradicate the Iraqi force from Kuwait, and Japan's financial support exemplified this understanding.

In the case of September 11, the answer was yes. Although Washington was aware of the impossibility of Japan's participation in combat, it regarded Japan's efforts to assist in the US War on Terror highly. Japan presented its "feasible" action without entering constitutional debates, allowing Japan to devise anti-terrorist measures and the JMSDF to undertake operations in the Indian Ocean. This shared strategic perspective of Japan was clear with its Military Emergency Law in December 2001.

The answer in the case of the March 11 earthquake was yes. Japan faced its greatest socio-economic crisis since World War II. The Obama Administration was quite aware of the restoration of Japan as critical for US strategic interest. In addition to the US offer of economic support, the 31MEU took the route from Southeast Asia to the Sea of Japan to demonstrate the strong US interest to "defend" Japan from China and North Korea, which might take advantage of the situation.

Did the Shared Collective Strategic Perspectives of the United States and Japan Influence the Process and Outcome of the Deliberations?

The answer in the Persian Gulf War was positive; there were active inter-governmental interactions concerning the war through various channels in both Washington and Tokyo. The failed efforts of the UNPKO bill passage in fall 1990 conversely paved the way for the JSDF's first dispatch overseas to the Persian Gulf in April 1991. This later led to the JSDF's participation in the United Nations peacekeeping operations on a regular basis.

In the case of the September 11 terrorist attacks, Koizumi consciously changed the policy-making process to realize the deployment of JMSDF vessels to the Indian Ocean. Koizumi's concentration of the decision-making power of the PMOR and "bypass" law-making strategy made it possible to enact fast anti-terrorist measures, and this legislation proved the change in Japanese policy since the Persian Gulf War.

In the case of the March 11 earthquake, the answer was yes. US-Japan cooperation became a model for future disaster relief operations by making the BCAT, formulating counter measures for nuclear accidents, and building close relationships between the local communities and the USFJ. This national level of recognition also extended to local communities in Japan.

Judgment

As shown in the summary of the results concerning the discourses and behaviors of the United States and Japan in the three case studies (see Table 6.1), this study found strong evidence showing a collective identity between the United States and Japan. In discourse, there was a linear change over time. The change from no development of a new vocabulary in the Persian Gulf War to the invention of "Operation Tomodachi" indicates the transformation of identity over the two

Table 6.1. Summary of Discourses and Behaviors of the United States and Japan

	Discourse	Behaviors			
	The development of a new vocabulary	Did the United States and Japan Act as partners?	Did the United States and Japan have explicit collective interests or a common good?	Did the United States and Japan have collective strategic perspectives?	Did the shared collective strategic perspectives of the United States and Japan influence the process and outcome of the deliberations?
The Persian Gulf War (1990–1)	No	Yes	Yes	Mixed	Yes
The September 11 terrorist attacks (2001)	Mixed	Yes	Yes	Yes	Yes
The March 11 Tohoku Earthquake (2011)	Yes	Yes	Yes	Yes	Yes

decades. Concerning behavior, except for the answer to the third question in the case of the Persian Gulf War, all answers to the inquiries in all cases were positive. Hence, this study judges the US-Japan relationship to represent a security community. Since this study confirmed the strong collective identity of the two countries, the community has reached the phase of maturity of evolution (Adler and Barnett, 1998b: 55–7). I found several important features of the relations between the two countries as a security community.

First, there is a strongly shared sense of others. As opposed to the "others" represented by Saddam Hussein (Iraq), Osama bin Laden, and actions in the 1995 Great Hanshin Earthquake, Japan had a strong sense of belonging to the group of countries sharing norms of democracy, liberty, peace, and humanity. This reinforced the peaceful change of US-Japan relations through the change of their policy-makers' common consciousness of collaborative endeavors to overcome crises, leading to institutional and legal changes. Japan's dispatch overseas of the JSDF to the Persian Gulf War in 1991 and the Indian Ocean in 2001 transcending constitutional constraints would not have been achieved without a sense of others. The overseas military deployment proves that a strong sense of others has gradually become anchored among Japanese policy-makers and law-makers within a decade.

The shared sense of others also somewhat altered the image of the USFJ. The Okinawa base issue has traditionally been the only lens for perceiving the USFJ since the end of World War II, and it has hampered the nurturing of a collective identity between Japan and the US. The unresolved issue of the return of the Futenma air base and much media coverage of crimes and accidents caused by the USFJ have continuously presented a negative image to the Japanese public and even made the public downplay the role of the USFJ in defending Japan. Nevertheless, the March 11 Tohoku Earthquake changed this. The past of the US as "other" was overcome, to some degree.

Second, there was a powerful community of practice in the US-Japan relationship that played an important role in enhancing the countries' shared sense of belonging and sense of other. By clarifying who they are and who they are not in the salience of the hierarchy in facing common crisis, the US-Japan community of practice successfully promoted peaceful change in the political segment outside of the community to devise anti-Hussein policy, anti-terrorism measurements, and disaster relief operations. Such a transnational community impressively informs us of the force of nurturing transnational conscience and expanding identity beyond national boundaries.

The Future of Security Community Studies

What is the future of security community studies? First, studies obviously require more geographic diversity in case studies. Studies must be conducted on US alignments in the Asia-Pacific region, i.e., US-South Korean, US-Philippine, US-Taiwanese, US-Australian, and US-New Zealand relations. Likewise, further research on Japan's relations with those US security partners would expand the horizon of security community studies, as well. Furthermore, researchers should extend study to transnational relations in Africa, Latin America, and the Middle East.

Second, security community studies need to inquire into bilateral relations. For example, China–Russia relations might be an interesting case. Their bilateral relations tend to be characterized as conflicting rather than cooperative. Nevertheless, those countries, possessing large populations and vast territorial space, have not often resorted to large-scale war in the past. Through such studies, IR scholars can obtain new knowledge and add to what we have accumulated up to the present.

Third, theoretical developments concerning the security community itself are still required. As the notion of the security community has been developed in fusion with constructivism, great emphasis has been placed on the collective identity and sense of others. This was perhaps inevitable because the importance of the "we-feeling" has been at the core of the security community model in accordance with its theoretical genealogy from Deutsch. Nevertheless, this notion might apply to a different type of danger from that considered in alliance theory. While research from the alliance theory perspective considers game theory, theory on the security community acknowledges the sharp contrast between "us" and "others" or between "friend" and "enemy" that is based on deep ideological discrepancies. In using the security community model, it is easily possible to draw a dichotomy between us and others that excludes fascist or communist regimes of the past. This study was not free from this danger when it showed Japan's cooperation in the US War on Terror. Japan has been now facing the rise of China. Japan will be more likely to seek to draw its sharp difference with it through geopolitics, domestic-social norms, and Asian regional integration (Sakai, 2017). This is an inside-outside dichotomy (Walker, 1992) in a country's foreign relations. It could represent inner peace within a security community and outer anarchy outside the community.

Nevertheless, I believe that this was not the theoretical intent of Deutsch. Rather, it was how the expansion of the "we-feeling" was possible. This is the reason why he chose the quantitative method to gauge the amount of transnational interactions. We now live in the age of globalization with webs of transportations, finance, trade, and internet that are far denser than those of Deutsch's time. For further theoretical development on the security community, IR scholars must find out how the expansion of the we-feeling or collective identity occurs, transcending "the clash of civilizations" (Huntington, 1996) or "the clash of ideas" (Owen, 2010).

Conclusion

This concluding chapter summarized the results of the three case studies. After the examination of discourse and behaviors in all cases, I judged the United States–Japan relationship to represent that of a security community. There was a strong sense of others in contrast with Saddam Hussein, Osama bin Laden, and Japan's own past. The existence of a community of practice of the United States and Japan played an important role in enhancing their collective identity in facing common crises. Lastly, this chapter noted the necessity of further theoretical development of the security community considering geographic diversity and other bilateral case studies. In addition, I argued that security community studies need to process how the we-feeling occurs so that our understanding of international relations (IR) will not fall into the dichotomy of "us" and "others."

Bibliography

Acharya, Amitav. (1998). "Collective Identity and Conflict Management in Southeast Asia," in *Security Communities*, edited by Emanuel Adler and Michael Barnett (Cambridge: Cambridge University Press), 198–227.

Acharya, Amitav. (2001). *Constructing a Security Community in Southeast Asia: ASEAN and the Problem of Regional Order* (London: Routledge).

Adler, Emanuel. (1991). "Cognitive Evolution: A Dynamic Approach for the Study of International Relations and Their Progress," in *Progress in Postwar International Relations*, edited by Emanuel Adler and Beverly Crawford (New York: Columbia University Press), 43–88.

Adler, Emanuel. (1997a). "Seizing the Middle Ground: Constructivism in World Politics," *European Journal of International Relations* 3: 319–63.

Adler, Emanuel. (1997b). "Imagined (Security) Communities: Cognitive Regions n International Relations," *Millennium: Journal of International Studies* 26(2): 249–77.

Adler, Emanuel. (1998a). "Seeds of Peaceful Change: the OSCE's Security Community-building Model," in *Security Communities*, edited by Emanuel Adler and Michael Barnett (Cambridge: Cambridge University Press), 119–60.

Adler, Emanuel. (1998b). "Condition(s) of Peace," *Review of International Studies* 28(5), 165–92.

Adler, Emanuel. (2005). *Communitarian International Relations: The Foundations of International Relations* (London: Routlege).

Adler, Emanuel. (2008). "The Spread of Security Communities: Communities of Practice, Self-Restraint, and NATO's Post-Cold War Transformation," *European Journal of International Relations* 14(2): 195–230.

Adler, Emanuel and Beverly Crawford (eds). (1991). *Progress in Postwar International Relations* (New York: Columbia University Press).

Adler, Emmanuel and Michael Barnett. (1998a). "Security Communities in Theoretical Perspective," in *Security Communities*, edited by Emanuel Adler and Michael Barnett (Cambridge: Cambridge University Press): 3–28.

Adler, Emanuel and Michael Barnett. (1998b). "A Framework for the Study of Security Communities," in *Security Communities*, edited by Emanuel Alder and Michael Barnett (Cambridge: Cambridge University Press): 29–65.

Adler, Emanuel and Michael Barnett (eds). (1998c). *Security Communities* (New York: Cambridge University Press).

Adams, Gordon and Stephen A. Cain. (1990, September 9). "Yes, We Still Need Defense Cuts; The Gulf Crisis Is No Excuse for a Retreat on Spending Reduction," *The Washington Post*, p. D2.

Anderson, Benedict. (2016). *Imagined Communities: Reflections on the Origin and Spread of Nationalism*, revised edition (London: Verso).

Apple, R. W. Jr. (1990). "Confrontation in the Gulf: U.S. May Send Saudis a Force of 50,000; Iraq Proclaims Kuwait's Annexation; Bush Draws 'Line'," *The New York Times*, August 9, Section A: 1.

Arase, David. (2007). "Japan, the Active State?: Security Policy after 9/11," *Asian Survey* 47(4): 560–83.

Armacost, Michael H. (1996). *Friends or Rivals?: The Insider's Account of U.S.-Japan Relations* (New York: Columbia University Press).

Asahi Shimbun. (1990, August 6), Evening Edition.

Asahi Shimbun. (1990, August 7).

Asahi Shimbun. (1990, August 10).

Asahi Shimbun. (1990, August 14), Evening Edition.

Asahi Shimbun. (1990, October 1).

Asahi Shimbun. (1990, August 29).

Asahi Shimbun. (1990, September 29), Evening Edition.

Asahi Shimbun. (1990, October 16),

Asahi Shimbun. (1990, October 17).

Asahi Shimbun. (1990, November 29).

Asahi Shimbun. (1991, January 19).

Asahi Shimbun. (1991, January 18).

Asahi Shimbun. (1991, January 19).

Asahi Shimbun. (1991, January 23).

Asahi Shimbun. (1991, January 24).

Asahi Shimbun. (1991, March 1).

Asahi Shimbun. (1991, March 12): Evening Edition.

Asahi Shimbun. (1991, March 15).

Asahi Shimbun. (1991, March 16).

Asahi Shimbun. (1991, April 11).

Asahi Shimbun. (1991, April 12).

Asahi Shimbun. (1991, April 24).

Asahi Shimbun. (1991, April 25).

Asahi Shimbun. (1991, April 27).

Asahi Shimbun. (2001, September 12).

Asahi Shimbun. (2001, September 12), Evening Edition.

Asahi Shimbun. (2001, September 13).

Asahi Shimbun. (2001, September 13), Evening Edition.

Asahi Shimbun. (2001, September 14).

Asahi Shimbun. (2001, September 16).

Asahi Shimbun. (2001, September 18).

Asahi Shimbun. (2001, September 19), Evening Edition.

Asahi Shimbun. (2001, September 20).
Asahi Shimbun. (2001, September 21).
Asahi Shimbun. (2001, September 25).
Asahi Shimbun. (2001, September 26), Evening Edition.
Asahi Shimbun. (2001, September 27).
Asahi Shimbun. (2001, September 27), Evening Edition.
Asahi Shimbun. (2001, October 6).
Asahi Shimbun. (2001, October 5).
Asahi Shimbun. (2001, October 19).
Asahi Shimbun. (2001, October 21).
Asahi Shimbun. (2001, November 9), Evening Edition.
Asahi Shimbun. (2002, February 16), Evening Edition.
Asahi Shimbun. (2002, February 19), Evening Edition.
Asahi Shimbun. (2002, November 9), Evening Edition.
Asahi Shimbun. (2011, March 11).
Asahi Shimbun. (2011, March 11), Evening Edition.
Asahi Shimbun. (2011, March 12).
Asahi Shimbun. (2011, March 14).
Asahi Shimbun. (2011, March 16), Evening Edition.
Asahi Shimbun. (2011, March 18).
Asahi Shimbun. (2011, March 18), Evening Edition.
Asahi Shimbun. (2011, March 21).
Asahi Shimbun. (2011, March 23).
Asahi Shimbun. (2011, March 26).
Asahi Shimbun. (2011, April 1).
Asahi Shimbun. (2011, April 2).
Asahi Shimbun. (2011, April 5).
Asahi Shimbun. (2011, April 7).
Asahi Shimbun. (2011, April 10).
Asahi Shimbun. (2011, April 16).
Asahi Shimbun. (2011, April 18).
Asahi Shimbun. (2011, April 22), Evening Edition.
Asahi Shimbun. (2011, May 22).
Attinà, Fulvio. (2000) "Partnership and Security: Some Theoretical and Empirical Reasons for Positive Developments in the Euro-Mediterranean Area," *Special Edition Euro-Mediterranean Partnership.* JMWP no. 27.00, Archive of European Integration (AEI). http://aei.pitt.edu/400/
Barnett, Michael and F. Gregory Gause III. (1998). "Caravans in Opposite Directions: Society, State and the Development of a Community in the Gulf Cooperation Council," in *Security Communities*, edited by Emanuel Adler and Michael Barnett (Cambridge: Cambridge University Press), 161–97.
BBC Monitoring Asia Pacific (2011, April 15, 2017). Transcript source: Kyodo News Service, Tokyo, in Engish, 1122GMT.
BBC Monitoring Asia Pacific (2011, April 17, 2017). Transcript, source: Kyodo News Service, Tokyo, in English, 0438GMT.

Bellamy, Alex J. (2004). *Security Communities and Their Neighbors: Regional Fortresses or Global Integrators?* (New York: Palgrave Macmillan).

Berger, Thomas. (1996). "Norms, Identity, and National Security in Germany and Japan," in *The Culture of National Security: Norms and Identity in World Politics*, edited by Peter J. Katzenstein (New York: Columbia University Press), 317–56.

Berger, Thomas. (1998). *Cultures of Antimilitarism: National Security in Germany and Japan* (Baltimore, ML: The Johns Hopkins University Press).

Blustein, Paul. (1990, September 14). "Japan Offers New Gulf Aids; $4 Billion to Help Economics, U.S.-Led Force," *The Washington Post*: A1.

Brown, David. (2003). *Palmerston and the Politics of Foreign Policy, 1846–1855* (Manchester: Manchester University Press).

Burgess, John and T. R. Reid. (1990). "U.S. Critics Not Satisfied With Japan's $4 Billion Gulf Contribution," *The Washington Post*, October 6: A24.

Bush, George. (1990). *Address Before a Joint Session of the Congress on the Persian Gulf Crisis and the Federal Budget Deficit*, September 11, 1990.

Buzan, Bary, Ole Wæver, and Jaap de Wilde. (1998). *Security: A New Framework for Analysis* (Boulder, Co: Lynne Rienner).

Buzan, Barry and Lene Hansen (eds). (2009). *The Evolution of International Security Studies* (Cambridge: Cambridge University Press).

Brown, Michael E., Sean M. Lynn-Jones, and Steven E. Miller (eds). (1995). *The Perils of Anarchy: Contemporary Realism and International Security* (Cambridge, MA: The MIT Press).

Calabrese, John. (1992/1993). "Peaceful or Dangerous Collaborators?: China's Relations with the Gulf Countries," *Pacific Affairs* 65(4) (winter): 471–85.

Calabrese, John. (1998). "China and the Persian Gulf: Energy and Security," *Middle East Journal* 52(3) (summer): 351–66.

Calder, Kent E. (1988). "Japanese Foreign Economic Policy Formation: Explaining the 'Reactive State'," *World Politics* 40 (July): 517–41.

Catalinac, Amy. (2007). "Identity Theory and Foreign Policy: Explaining Japan's Responses to the 1991 Gulf War and the 2003 U.S. War in Iraq," *Politics and Policy* 35(1): 58–100.

Claiborne, William. (1990a, August 12). "Egyptian Troops Land in Saudi Arabia," *The Washington Post*: A1.

Claiborne, William. (1990b, August 15). "New Troops Take Places In Desert; Syrians Expected; Morocco and Egypt Bolster Contingent," *The Washington Post*: A12.

Cohen, Ira J. (1987). "Structuration Theory and Social Praxis," in *Social Theory Today* edited by Anthony Giddens and Jonathan Turner (Stanford, CA: Stanford University Press), 273–308.

Chau, Andrew. (2008). "Security Community and Southeast Asia: Australia, the US, and ASEAN's Counter-Terror Strategy," *Asian Survey* 48(4) (July/August): 629–49.

Checkel, Jeffery T. (1998). "The Constructivist Turn in International Relations Theory" *World Politics* 50(2) (January): 324–48.

Cronin, Bruce (1999). *Community Under Anarchy: Transnational Identity and the Evolution of Cooperation* (New York: Columbia University Press).

Defense Agency of Japan. (1990). *Defense of Japan 1990* (Tokyo: The Defense Agency).

Deutsch, Karl W., Sidney A. Burrell, Robert A. Kann, Maurice Lee, Jr., Martin Lichterman, Raymond E. Lindgren, Francis L. Loewenheim, and Richard W. Van Wagenen. (1957). *Political Community and the North Atlantic Area: International Organization in the Light of Historical Experience* (Princeton, NJ, Princeton University Press).

Deutsch, Karl W. (1978). *The Analysis of International Relations*, 2nd edition (Englewood Cliffs, NJ: Prentice-Hall).

Devroy, Ann. (1990, November 20). "Bush Hints Accord At Hand on Force; Shevardnadze Calls for U.N. 'to Take Stock'," *The Washington Post*: A1.

Dobbs, Michael. (1990, September 10). "Superpower Prestige on the Line; Former Foes Beginning New Era of International Cooperation," *The Washington Post*, September 10: A1.

Dower, John W. (2000). *Embracing Defeat: Japan in the Wake of World War II* (New York: W. W. Norton and Company).

Drozdiak, William. (1990a, August 8). "NATO Redefines Defense Role; Iraqi Invasion Forces Alliance to Take on New Security Mission," *The Washington Post*: A12.

Drozdiak, William. (1990b, September 1). "Allies Split On Military Aid to Gulf; Economic Assistance Is Less Divisive Issue," *The Washington Post*: A20.

Eckstein, Harry. (1975). "Case Study and Theory in Political Science," in *Handbook of Political Science Vol. 7, Strategies of Inquiry*, edited by Fred I. Greenstein and Nelson W. Polsby (Reading, CA: Addison-Wesley), 79–137.

Edelstein, David. (2002) "Managing Uncertainty: Beliefs about Intentions and the Rise of the Great Powers," *Security Studies* 12(1) (Autumn): 1–40.

Eldridge, Robert D. (ed.). (2016). *Tsugi no Shinsai ni Sonaeru Tameni: America Kaiheitai no "Tomodachi Sakusen" Keikensha ga Teigen Suru Gunmin Kyoroku no Atarashii Arikata* (Tokyo: Kindai Shobo Sha).

Eldridge, Robert D. (2017). *Tomodachi Sakusen: Kesennuma Oshima to Beigun Kaiheitai no Kiseki no Kizuna* (Tokyo: Shūei Sha).

Falk, Richard A. and Saul H. Mendlviz (eds). (1973). *Regional Politics and World Order* (San Francisco: W. H. Freeman).

Fisher, Marc. (1990a, August 10). "West German Troops to Remain Out of Gulf; Reunification Plans Will Take Priority," *The Washington Post*: A30.

Fisher, Marc. (1990b, August 14). "European Grope for Unified Response Toward Persian Gulf Threat; Bonn, Leery of Larger Role, Considers Joining Task Force," *The Washington Post*: A18.

Freund, Charles Paul. (1990). "The New Face of the Enemy; Hitler, Satellites, Children and Golf: The Art of Persuasion in an Age of Skepticism," *The Washington Post*, August 26: C1.

Garofano, John. (2002). "Power, Institutions, and the ASEAN Regional Forum: A Security Community for Asia?" *Asian Survey* 42(3) (May/June): 502–21.

Gill, Bates. (2002). "September 11 and Northeast Asia: Change and Uncertainty in Regional Security," *The Brookings Review* 20(3) (summer): 43–6.

Gilpin, Robert. (1981). *War and Change in World Politics* (Cambridge: Cambridge University Press).

Glaser, Charles. (1995). "Realists as Optimists: Cooperation as Self-Help," in *The Perils of Anarchy: Contemporary Realism and International Security*, edited by Michael E. Brown, Sean M. Lynn-Jones, and Steven E. Miller (Cambridge, MA: The MIT Press), 377–417.

Glaser, Charles. (2010). *Rational Theory of International Politics: The Logic of Competition and Cooperation* (Princeton, NJ: Princeton University Press).

Gonzalez, Guadalupe and Stephen Haggard. (1998). "The United States and Mexico: A Pluralistic Security Community?" in *Security Communities*, edited by Emanuel Adler and Michael Barnett (Cambridge: Cambridge University Press), 295–332.

Goodby, James, Petrus Buwalda, and Dmitri Trenin. (2002). *A Strategy for Stable Peace: Toward a Euroatlatntic Security Community* (Washington, DC: United Institute for Peace).

Goodby, James E. and Benoit Morel (eds) (1993). *The Limited Partnership: Building a Russian-U.S. Security Community* (Oxford: Oxford University Press).

Goshko, John M. (1990, August 10). "U.N. Declares Annexation of Kuwait 'Void'; Iraq Closes Borders, Bars Exit of Foreigners; Multinational Military Force A Possibility," *The Washington Post*: A1.

Gould, D. Harry. (1998). "What Is at Stake in the Agent-Structure Debate," in *International Relations in a Constructed World*, edited by Vendulka Kubálková, Nicholas Onuf, and Paul Kowert (Armonk, NY: M. E. Sharpe), 79–98.

Greenstein, Fred I. and Nelson W. Polsby. (1975). *Handbook of Political Science Vol. 7, Strategies of Inquiry* (Reading, CA: Addison-Wesley).

GRIPS (National Graduate Institute for Policy Studies). (2005). *Kuriyama Takakazu-Oral History: Wangan Sensō to Nihon Gaikō*, edited by C. O. E Oral and Seisaku Kenkyū Purojekuto (Tokyo: GRIPS), 39.

Haas, Ernst B. and Allen S. Whiting. (1956). *Dynamics of International Relations* (New York: McGraw-Hill Book Company).

Haas, Ernst B. (1973). "The Study of Regional Integration: Reflections on the Joy and Anguish of Pretheorizing," in *Regional Politics and World Order*, edited by Richard A. Falk and Saul H. Mendlviz (San Francisco, CA: W. H. Freeman).

Hanai, Hitoshi and Koki Asakawa (eds). (1995). *Sengo Nichibei Kankei no Kiseki* (Tokyo: Keisō Shobō).

Hara, Yoshihisa. (1992). *Nichibei Kankei no Kōzu: Anpo Kaitei wo Kenshō Suru* (Tokyo: NHK Books).

Hara, Yoshihisa. (2005). *Yoshida Shigeru: Sonnō no Seijika* (Tokyo: Iwanami Shoten).

Harris, Lillian Craig. (1991). "The Gulf Crisis and China's Middle East Dilemma," *Pacific Review* 4(2): 116–25.

Hart, B. H. Liddle. (1967). *Strategy*, 2nd ed. (New York: Frederik Praeger).

Hegel, G. W. F. (1967). *Philosophy of Right*, translated by T. M. Knox (New York: Oxford University Press).

Hemmer, Christopher and Peter J. Katzenstein. (2008). "Why Is There No NATO in Asia?: Collective Identity, Regionalism, and the Origins of Multilateralism," in *Rethinking Japanese Security: Internal and External Dimensions*, edited by Peter J. Katzenstein (London: Routledge), 185–211.

Hewitt, John. (1976). *Self and Society: A Symbolic Interactionist Social Psychology* (Boston: Allyn and Bacon).

Hisae, Masahiko. (2002). *9/11 to Nihon Gaikō* (Tokyo: Kodansha).

Hobbes, Thomas. (1996). *Leviathan*, revised student edition, edited by Richard Tuck (New York: Cambridge University Press).

Hoffman, David. (1990, August 9). "U.S. Pushes Contacts With Iraq's Enemies, Syria and Iran," *The Washington Post*: A33.

Hogg, Michael and Dominic Abrams. (1988). *Social Identifications: A Social Psychology of Intergroup Relations and Group Process* (New York: Routledge).

Huo, Hwei-ling. (1992). "Patterns of Behavior in China's Foreign Policy: The Gulf Crisis and Beyond," *Asian Survey* 32(3) (March): 263–76.

Huntington, Samuel P. (1996). *The Clash of Civilizations and the Remaking of World Order* (New York: Touchstone).

Hurrell, Andrew. (1998). "An Emerging Security Community in South America?" in *Security Communities*, edited by Emanuel Adler and Michael Barnett (Cambridge: Cambridge University Press), 228–64.

Iijima, Isao. (2006). *Koizumi Kantei Hiroku* (Tokyo: Nihon Keizai Shimbun Sha).

Iijima, Isao. (2007). *Jitsuroku Koizumi Gaiko* (Tokyo: Nihon Keizai Shimbun Sha).

Imai, Masakazu. (2012). "Higashi Nihon Daishinsai ni okeru Jieitai no Katsudo Nichibei Kyoryoku: Jieitai no Saigai Haken to Beigun no Tomodachi Sakusen no Kadai," *Rippo to Chosa* 329 (June): 66–71.

Ikenberry, G. John and Michael Mastanduno (eds). (2003). *International Relations Theory and the Asia-Pacific* (New York: Columbia University Press).

Ikenberry, G. John. (2006). *Libeal Order and Imperial Ambition: Essays on American Power and World Politics* (Cambridge: Polity Press).

Ikenberry, G. John and Takashi Inoguchi. (2007). *The Uses of Institutions: The U.S., Japan and Governance in East Asia* (New York: Palgrave).

Ikenberry, G. John. (2011). *Liberal Leviathan: The Origins, Crisis, and Transformation of the American World Order* (Princeton, NJ: Princeton University Press).

International Business Times. (2011, March 12), custom wire.

International Herald Tribune. (2011, March 23).

Iokibe, Makoto, and Taizō Miyagi (eds). (2013). *Hashimoto Ryūtarō Gaikō Kaiko Roku* (Tokyo: Iwanami Shoten).

Ishihara, Nobuo. (1997). *Shushō Kantei no Ketsudan: Naikaku Kanbō Fuku Chōkan Ishihara Nobuo no 2600 Nichi* (Tokyo: Chuōkōron Sha), 64–5.

Ishikawa, Taku. (2002). "Alliances in Security Communities: Theoretical Perspectives on Compatibility," in *An Alliance for Engagement: Building*

Cooperation in Security Relations with China, edited by Benjamin L. Self and Jeffery W. Thompson (Washington, DC: The Henry L. Stimson), 30–53.

Japan Economic Newswire. (2011, March 29), newswire, 1535GMT.

Japanese Ministry of Defense. (2011). "Higashi nihon daishinsai eno taio ni kansuru kyoukun jiko ni tusite: chukan tori matome," 18. Accessed March 15, 2018. www.mod.go.jp/j/approach/defense/saigai/pdf/k_chukan.pdf.

Japanese Ministry of Foreign Affairs. (2011). "Nichibei Anzen Hosho Kyogi Iinkai Bunsho, 'Higashi Nihon Daishinsai eno taio ni Okeru Kyoryoku,' June 21, U.S. Secretary of State Clinton, U.S. Secretary of Defense Gates, Japanese Minister of Foreign Affairs Matsumoto, and Japanese Minister of Defense Kitazawa." Accessed March 15, 2018. www.mofa.go.jp/mofaj/area/usa/hosho/pdfs/joint1106_03.pdf.

The Japan Times. (2012, March 3).

Jervis, Robert. (1976). *Perception and Misperception in International Politics* (Princeton, NJ: Princeton University Press).

Jiji Press Ticker Service. (2011, March 15), newswire.

Kabashima, Ikuo and Gill Steel. (2007). "The Koizumi Revolution," *Political Science and Politics* 40(1) (January): 79–84.

Kato, Akira. (1995). "Posuto Reisen: Nichibei Masatsu no Jidai," in *Sengo Nichibei Kankei no Kiseki*, edited by Hitoshi Hanai and Koki Asakawa (Tokyo: Keisō Shobō), 199–223.

Katzenstein, Peter J. (ed.). (1996). *The Culture of National Security: Norms and Identity in World Politics* (New York: Columbia University Press).

Katzenstein,Peter J. (ed.). (2008). *Rethinking Japanese Security: Internal and External Dimensions* (London: Routledge).

Kavalski, Emilian. (2008). *Extending the European Security Community: Constructing Peace in the Balkans* (London: Tauris Academic Studies).

Kavalski, Emilian. (2014). "The Shadows of Normative Power in Asia: Framing the International Agency of China, India and Japan," *Pacific Focus* 29(3) (December): 303–28.

Kawasaki, Tsuyoshi. (2007). "Layering Institutions: The Logic of Japan's Institutional Strategy for Regional Security," in *The Uses of Institutions: The U.S., Japan and Governance in East Asia*, edited by John Ikenberry and Takashi Inoguchi (New York: Palgrave), 77–102.

Kegley, Charles W. and Eugene R. Wittkopf (eds). (1984). *The Global Agenda: Issues and Perspectives* (New York: Random House).

Kennan, George F. (1947). "The Source of Soviet Conducts," *Foreign Affairs*, June 19: 566–82.

Keohane, Robert O. (1984). *After Hegemony: Cooperation and Discord in the World Political Economy* (Princeton, NJ: Princeton University Press).

Keohane, Robert O. (1999). "Risk, Threat, and Security Institutions," in *Imperfect Unions: Security Institutions over Time and Space*, edited by Helga Haftendron, Robert O. Keohane, and Celeste Wallander (Oxford: Oxford University Press), 21–47.

Kitaoka, Shinichi. (2000). "Japan's Identity and What It Means," Japan Forum on International Relations.

Kratochwil, Friedrich V. (1989). *Rules, Norms and Decisions: On the Conditions of Practical and Legal Reasoning in International Relations and Domestic Affairs* (Cambridge: Cambridge University Press).

Kuriyama, Takakazu. (1991). "Waga Gaimushōan Hinome wo mizu," *Bungei Shunjū* 69 (January): 292–302.

Kuriyama, Takakazu. (1997). *Nichibei Dōmei: Hyōryū kara no Dakkyaku* (Tokyo: Nihon Keizai Shimbun Sha).

Kubálková, Vendulka, Nicholas Onuf and Paul Kowert (eds). (1998). *International Relations in a Constructed World*, edited by (Armonk, NY: M. E. Sharpe).

Kunimasa, Takeshige. (1999). *Wangan Sensō to yū Tenkaiten: Dōten Suru Nihon Seiji* (Tokyo: Iwanami Shoten).

Kupchan, Charles A. (2010). *How Enemies Become Friends: The Sources of Stable Peace* (Princeton, NJ: Princeton University Press).

Kuriyama, Takakazu. (1997). *Nichibei Dōmei: Hyōryū kara no Dakkyaku* (Tokyo: Nihon Keizai Shimbun Sha).

Kuroda, Yasumasa. (2001). *Japan's Middle East Policy: Fuzzy Nonbinary Process Model, in Japanese Foreign Policy in Asia and the Pacific: Domestic Interests, American Pressure, and Regional Integration*, edited by Akitoshi Miyashita and Yoichiro Sato (New York: Palgrave), 101–18.

Liska, George. (1962). *Nations in Alliance: The Limits of Interdependence* (Baltimore, ML: The Johns Hopkins Press).

Mattern, Janice Bially. (2001). "The Power Politics of Identity," *European Journal of International Relations* 7(3): 349–97.

Mead, George Herbert. (1934). *Mind, Self, and Society from the Standpoint of a Social Behaviorist* (Chicago: University of Chicago Press).

Mearsheimer, John. J. (1990). "Back to the Future: Instability in Europe After the Cold War," *International Security* 15(1), 5–56.

Midford, Paul. (2003). "Japan's Response to Terror: Dispatching the SDF to the Arabian Sea," *Asian Survey* 43(2): 329–51.

Ministry of Foreign Affairs (MOFA). (1957). *The Diplomatic Bluebook 1957* (Tokyo: Ministry of Foreign Affairs).

Miyashita, Akitoshi and Yoichiro Sato (eds). (2001). *Japanese Foreign Policy in Asia and the Pacific: Domestic Interests, American Pressure, and Regional Integration* (New York: Palgrave).

Mochizuki, M. Mike (ed.). (1997). *Toward a True Alliance: Restructuring U.S.-Japan Security Relations* (Washington, DC: Brookings Institution Press).

Morimoto, Satoshi. (1997). "A Tighter Japan-U.S. Alliance Based on Greater Trust," in *Toward a True Alliance: Restructuring U.S.-Japan Security Relations*, edited by Mike M. Mochizuki (Washington, DC: Brookings Institution Press), 137–48.

Morse, Edward L. (1972). "Transnational Economic Processes," in *Transnational Relations and World Politics*, edited by Robert O. Keohane and Joseph S. Nye (Cambridge, MA: Harvard University Press).

Moustakis, Fotios and Tracey C. German. (2009). *Securing Europe: Western Interventions towards a New Security Community* (London: Tauris Academic Studies).

Möller, Frank. (2003). "Capitalizing on Difference: A Security Community or/ as a Western Project," *Security Dialogue* 34(3), 315–28.

Möller, Frank. (2007). *Thinking Peaceful Change: Baltic Security Policies and Security Community Building* (Syracuse, NY: Syracuse University Press).

Muroyama, Yoshimasa. (1992a). *Nichibei Anpo Taisei: Reisengo no Anzen Hoshō Senryoku wo Kōsō Suru: Heiwa Kenpō Seitei kara Okinawa Henkan made* (Tokyo: Yuikaku).

Muryoyama, Yoshimasa. (1992b). *Nichibei Anpo Taisei: Reisengo no Anzen Hoshō Senyaku wo kōsō suru: Nixon Doctrine kara Wangan Sensō made* (Tokyo: Yūikaku).

Murata, Ryōhei. (2008). *Murata Ryōhei Kaisōroku: Sokoku no Saisei wo Jisedai ni Takushite*, Second Volume (Kyoto: Minerva Shobō).

The New Oxford Dictionary of English. (1998). Judy Pearsall (ed.) (Oxford: Oxford University Press).

The New York Times. (2011, March 23).

The New York Times. (2011, April 14).

Ngoma, Naison. (2005). *Prospects for a Security Community in Southern Africa: An Analysis of Regional Security in the Southern African Development Community* (Pretoria, South Africa: Institute for Security Studies).

Nye, Joseph S. and David A. Welch. (2013). *Understanding Global Conflict and Cooperation: An Introduction to Theory and History*, 8th edition (Boston: Pearson).

Oe, Kenzaburo. (1995). *Japan, the Ambiguous, and Myself* (Tokyo: Kodansha International).

Owen, John. (1997). *Liberal Peace and Liberal War: American Politics and International Security* (Cornell, NY: Cornell University Press).

Owen IV, John M. (2010). *The Clash of Ideas in World Politics: Transnational Networks, States, and Regime Change, 1510–2010* (Princeton, NJ: Princeton University Press).

Ozawa, Ichiro. (1993). *Nihon Kaizō Keikaku* (Tokyo: Kodansha).

Pascha, Werner and Bernhard Seliger (eds). (2011). *Towards a Northeast Asian Security Community: Implications for Korea's Growth and Economic Development* (New York: Springer).

Pervez, Muhammad Shoaib. (2013). *Security Community in South Asia: India-Pakistan* (London: Routledge).

Prime Miniser of Japan and His Cabinet. (2001). "Statement by Prime Minister Junichiro Koizumi at the Press Confernce, September 12." Accessed March 2, 2018. https://japan.kantei.go.jp/koizumispeech/2001/0912kaiken_e.html.

Prime Minister of Japan and His Cabinet. (2001). "Kanbō Chōkan Happyō: Sōri no tōnan azia hōmon no enki no ken ni tsuite, September 13." Accessed March 2, 2018. www.kantei.go.jp/jp/tyoukanpress/rireki/2001/09/13_p2.html.

Prime Miniser of Japan and His Cabinet. (2001). "Opening Statement by Prime Minister Junichiro Koizumi at the Press Conference, September 19." Accessed March 2, 2018. https://japan.kantei.go.jp/koizumispeech/2001/0919sourikaiken_e.html.

Prime Minister of Japan and His Cabinet. (2001). "G8 Heads of Government Statement, September 20." Accessed March 2, 2018. https://japan.kantei.go.jp/koizumispeech/2001/0920g8seimei_e.html.

Prime Minister of Japan and His Cabinet. (2001). "Remarks by Prime Minister Junichiro Koizumi at the Ceremony for All Victims of Terrorist Attacks in U.S. September 23." Accessed March 7, 2018. https://japan.kantei.go.jp/koizumispeech/2001/0923aisatu_e.html.

Prime Minister of Japan and His Cabinet. (2001). "Statement by Prime Minister Junichiro Koizumi, October 8." Accessed March 2, 2018. https://japan.kantei.go.jp/koizumispeech/2001/1008danwa_e.html.

Prime Minister of Japan and His Cabinet. (2001). "Statement by Prime Minister Junichiro Koizumi, October 29." Accessed March 2, 2018. https://japan.kantei.go.jp/koizumispeech/2001/1029danwa_e.html.

Prime Miniser of Japan and His Cabinet. (2001). "Kanbō Chōkan Kisha Kaiken, September 13." Accessed March 2, 2018. www.kantei.go.jp/jp/tyoukanpress/rireki/2001/09/13_p2.html.

Prime Minister of Japan and His Cabinet. (2011). "Japan's Road to Recovery and Re-birth (Op-ed by Prime Minister Kan to Washington Post), April 15, 2011." Accessed March 15, 2018. https://japan.kantei.go.jp/kan/statement/201104/15kikou_WP_e.html.

Pyle, Kenneth B. (2007). *Japan Rising: The Resurgence of Japanese Power and Purpose* (New York: Public Affairs).

Reid, T. R. (1990a, August 14). "Kaifu Cancels Trip to Arabian Peninsula; Japanese Diplomats Feared Journey Could Look Like Oil-Buying Expedition," *The Washington Post*: A16.

Reid, T. R. (1990b, October 16). "Kaifu Makes Troops Proposals; Japanese Premier Offers Bill Allowing Support Contingent in Gulf," *The Washington Post*: A18.

Reiter, Dan. (1996). *Crucible of Belief: Learning, Alliances, and World Wars* (Ithaca, NY: Cornell University Press).

Remnick, David. (1990). "Soviets Condemn Annexation, Consider U.N. Military Role," *The Washington Post*, August 10: A25.

Risse-Kappen, Thomas. (1995). *Cooperation among Democracies: The European Influence on U.S. Foreign Policy* (Princeton, NJ: Princeton University Press).

Risse-Kappen, Thomas. (1996). "Collective Identity in a Democratic Community: the Case of NATO," in *The Culture of National Security: Norms and Identity in World Politics*, edited by Peter J. Katzenstein (New York: Columbia University Press), 357–99.

Rose, Gideon. (1998). "Neoclassical Realism and Theories of Foreign Policy," *World Politics* 51 (October): 144–72.

Ruggie, John Gerald. (1998). *Constructing the World Polity: Essays on International Institutionalization* (London: Routlege).

Rumelili, Bahar. (2007). *Constructing Regional Community and Order in Europe and Southeast Asia* (Hampshire: Palgrave Macmillan).

Russet, Bruce. (1993). *Grasping Democratic Peace: Principles for A Post-Cold War World* (Princeton, NJ: Princeton University Press).

Sakai, Hidekazu. (2003). "The End of Comprehensive Security?: The Evolution of Japanese Security Policy in the Post-September 11-Terrorism World," *Indian Journal of Asian Affairs* 16(1–2) (June/December): 71–98.

Sakai, Hidekazu. (2004). "Anzen Hoshō Kyōdōtai to Shite no Nichibei Kankei," *Hōsei Rongyō* 41(1) (November): 270–82.

Sakai, Hidekazu and Yoichiro Sato (eds). (2017). *Re-rising Japan: Its Strategic Power in International Relations* (New York: Peter Lang).

Sakai, Hidekazu. (2017). "Introduction: Is Japan Falling or Rerising?" in *Re-rising Japan: Its Strategic Power in International Relations*, edited by Hidekazu Sakai and Yoichiro Sato (New York: Peter Lang).

Sakamoto, Yoshikazu. (1987). "The International Context of the Occupation of Japan," in *Democratizing Japan: The Allied Occupation*, edited by Robert E. Ward and Yoshikazu Sakamoto (Honolulu: University of Hawaii Press), 42–75.

Samuels, Richard J. (2007). *Securing Japan: Tokyo's Grand Strategy and the Future of East Asia* (Ithaca, NY: Cornell University Press).

Schweller, Randall L. (1996). "Neorealism's Status-Quo Bias: What Security Dilemma?" In *Realism: Restatement and Renewal*, edited by Benjamin Frankel (London: Frank Cass).

Schweller, Randall L. (1998). *Deadly Imbalances: Tripolarity and Hitler's Strategy of World Conquest* (New York: Columbia University Press).

Seliger, Bernhard and Werner Pascha (eds). (2011). *Towards a Northeast Asian Security Community: Implications for Korea's Growth and Economic Development* (New York: Springer).

Shibutani, Tamotsu. (1955). "Reference Groups as Perspectives," *American Journal of Sociology* 60(6) (May): 562–9.

Shichor, Yitzhak. (1992). "China and the Middle East Since Tiananmen," *The Annals of the American Academy of Political and Social Science*, 519 (January): 86–100.

Shinoda, Tomohito. (2005). "Japan's Cabinet Secretariat and Its Emergence as Core Executive," *Asian Survey* 45(5): 800–21.

Shinoda, Tomohito. (2004). *Kantei Gaiko: Seiji Leadership no Yukue* (Tokyo: Asahi Shimbun Sha).

Shinoda, Tomohito. (2006). *Reisengo no Nihon Gaiko: Anzen Hosho Seisaku no Kokunai Seiji Katei* (Kyoto: Minerva Shobo).

Shore, Sean M. (1998). "No Fences Make Good Neighbors: the Development of the US-Canadian Security Community, 1871–1940," in *Security Communities*, edited by Emanuel Adler and Michael Barnett (Cambridge: Cambridge University Press), 333–66.

Snyder, Glenn H. (1997). *Alliance Politics* (Ithaca, NY: Cornell University Press).

Stryker, Sheldon. (1980). *Symbolic Interactionism: A Social Structural Version* (Menlo Park, CA: Benjamin/Cummings).

Tamamoto, Masaru. (2003). "Ambiguous Japan: Japanese National Identity at Century's End," in *International Relations Theory and the Asia-Pacific*, edited by G. John Ikenberry and Michael Mastanduno (New York: Columbia University Press), 191–212.

Tanba, Minoru. (2011). *Waga Gaikō Jinsei* (Tokyo: Chūō Kōron Sha).

Teshima, Ryūichi. (1993). *1991 Nen Nihon no Haiboku, Tokyo: Shinchōcha, 1993.*

United States Army. (2011). "9th AML deploys to Japan," April 14. Accessed March 15, 2018. www.army.mil/article/54919/9th_AML_deploys_to_Japan.

United States Air Force. (2011). "Radiation assessment team surveys Sendai Airport," April 5. Accessed March 15, 2018. www.pacaf.af.mil/News/Article-Display/Article/594258/radiation-assessment-team-surveys-sendai-airport/.

The Washington Post. (2001, April 17).

The Washington Post. (2011, April 17).

Walker, R. B. J. (1992). *Inside/Outside: International Relations as Political Theory* (Cambridge: Cambridge University Press).

Waltz, Kenneth N. (1979). *Theory of International Politics* (New York: McGraw-Hill).

Waltz, Kenneth N. (2000). "Structural Realism after the Cold War," *International Security* 25(1) (summer): 5–41.

Wendt, Alexander. (1992). "Anarchy is What States Make of It: the Social Construction of Power Politics," *International Organization* 46(2) (spring): 391–425.

Wendt, Alexander. (1994). "Collective Identity Formation and the International State," *American Political Science Review* 88(2) (June): 384–96.

Wendt, Alexander. (1999). *Social Theory of International Politics* (Cambridge: Cambridge University Press).

Weber, Steve. (1993). "Shaping the Postwar Balance of Power: Multilateralism in NATO," in *Multilateralism Matters: The Theory and Praxis of an Institutional Form*, edited by John Gerald Ruggie (New York: Columbia University Press), 233–92.

Wæver, Ole. (1998). "Insecurity, Security, and Asecurity in the West European Non-war Community," in *Security Communities*, edited by Emanuel Adler and Michael Barnett (Cambridge: Cambridge University Press), 69–118.

White House. (2011). "News Conference by the President," 12:33EST, March 11, 2011, South Court Auditorium.

Williams, Michael C. and Iver B. Neumann. (2000). "From Alliance to Security Community: NATO, Russia, and the Power of Identity," *Millennium: Journal of International Studies* 29(2), 357–87.

Wines, Michael. (1990, August 23). "Confrontation in the Gulf; Saudis Plan to Supply U.S. With Fuel for Military Use," *The New York Times*: A14.

Wohlforth, William Curti. (1993). *The Elusive Balance: Power and Perceptions during the Cold War* (Ithaca, NY: Cornell University Press).

Yamaguchi, Jirō. (1992). "The Gulf War and the Transformation of Japanese Constitutional Politics," *Journal of Japanese Studies* 18(1): 155–72.

Yomiuri Shimbun. (1991, January 17), Evening Edition.

Yomiuri Shimbun. (1991, January 18).

Yomiuri Shimbun. (1991, January 19), Evening Edition.
Yomiuri Shimbun. (1991, January 24).
Yomiuri Shimbun. (1991, January 25).
Yomiuri Shimbun. (1991, March 15).
Yomiuri Shimbun. (2011, March 13).
Yomiuri Shimbun. (2011, March 14).
Yomiuri Shimbun. (2011, March 15).
Yomiuri Shimbun. (2011, March 18), Evening Edition.
Yomiuri Shimbun. (2011, March 24).
Yomiuri Shimbun. (2011, March 28).
Yomiuri Shimbun. (2011, March 30).
Yomiuri Shimbun. (2011, April 1).
Yomiuri Shimbun. (2011, April 2), Evening Edition.
Yomiuri Shimbun. (2011, April 4), Evening Edition
Yomiuri Shimbun. (2011, April 9).
Yomiuri Shimbun. (2011, April 9), Evening Edition.
Yomiuri Shimbun. (2011, April 13).
Yomiuri Shimbun. (2011, April 15), Evening Edition.
Yomiuri Shimbun. (2011, April 21).
Yomiuri Shimbun. (2011, April 21), Evening Edition.
Yomiuri Shimbun. (2011, May 20).
Yomiuri Shimbun Seijibu. (2006). *Gaikō wo Kenka ni Shita Otoko: Koizumi Gaikō 200 Nichi no Shinjitsu* (Tokyo: Shinchosha).
Zakaria, Fareed. (1998). *From Wealth to Power: The Unusual Origins of America's World Role* (Princeton, NJ: Princeton University Press).
Zupančic, Rok and Miha Hribernik. (2014). "Discovering' Normative Power as a State Strategy in the Framework of Security, Foreign, and Defense Policy: The Case of Japan," *Philippine Political Science Journal* 35(1): 78–97.
Zupančic, Rok. (2013, December). "Normative Power Japan: The European Union's Ideational Successor or Another 'Contribution in Terms'?" *Romanian Journal of Political Science*: 106–36.

Index

Abrams, Dominic 6
Acharya, Amitav 27n3
Adler, Emanuel 7, 13, 15, 16–17, 19,
  29, 46n1
Afghanistan 12, 52, 57, 58, 62
Aguilar, George 73
All Japan Seamen's Union 43
"alliance dependence" 33
altruism 1, 5, 6, 15
amalgamated security communities 8
American Revolution 10
anti-militarism, norm of 31
Apple, R. W. Jr. 38
ARF (ASEAN Regional
  Forum) 5, 76
Armacost, Michael 33, 40, 42, 43
Armitage, Richard 52–3
Asahi Shimbun (newspaper) 36, 37,
  52, 57, 58
Aso, Taro 51

Baker, James 35, 38, 41, 42
Bansho, Koichiro 78
Barnett, Michael 13, 15, 16–17,
  29, 46n1
behaviors and collective identity:
  mutual predictability of 19; in
  Persian Gulf War 30–3, 39–45; and
  September 11 attacks 58–66, 70–1;
  theory of 16, 17–19, 23, 24, 26; and
  Tohoku Earthquake 75–82, 85–7
Bentsen, Lloyd 39
Berger, Thomas 22, 31
Bolton, John 57
Brady, Nick 41, 44
Brown, David 3

Burgess, John 39
Burke, Thom 74, 78
Bush, George 34–5, 36–7, 38, 41,
  52, 56, 58

Calder, Kent E. 31
Campbell, Kurt 52–3, 56–7
Catalinac, Amy 32
Chaplin, Robert 51–2
China 10, 23, 31, 81, 90
classical realism 70
Clinton, Hillary 73, 74, 79
Cold War 4, 9, 10, 21, 22, 32, 70
collective identity 7; and changes
  24–5; detection of 26; and
  emergency 25; and shared historical
  experiences 23; stages of 13; theory
  of 17, 19, 20–5; vocabulary of 26
collective norms 16
colonization 10, 23
communication 3, 14–15, 16, 18
community of practice 19–20, 27, 55,
  64, 84, 86, 89
constructivism 6–7, 15, 19, 90
cooperation 3, 4–5, 34
Cronin, Bruce 6, 7, 23, 26

de Michelis, Gianni 35
defensive realism 3–4
Democratic Party of Japan (DPJ) 72
Deutsch, Karl W. et al. (1957) 7–8, 9,
  13n3, 14, 15, 16, 19, 27n2, 28n4
Diego Garcia 49
discourses and collective identity 26,
  32, 34–9, 51–8, 72–5, 83–5
Dobbs, Michael 34

Taliban 49
Tanaka, Makiko 59
Tanba, Minoru 40–1, 44, 45
Teshima, Ryūichi 47n7
Thatcher, Margaret 35
Tohoku Earthquake 25, 68–91;
  behaviors 75–82, 85–7; discourses
  72–5; evacuation 69
transnational identity 7, 24
tsunami 68, 75, 77
Tsuno, Osamu 60

UN (United Nations): Japan
  membership of 24; peacekeeping
  operations (PKOs) 45; and Persian
  Gulf War 31, 32
UNCC (United Nations Cooperation
  Corps) 37, 41
United Kingdom 6, 20, 24
United Nations Peacekeeping
  Operations Law (UNPKO Law) 62
UNPC (United Nations Peace
  Cooperation) 37–8, 41, 44
US (United States): amalgamated
  security community 8; British
  colonization 10; East Asian forces
  49; Group of Six 24; hegemony 6;
  hub-and-spoke alliances 9; Joint
  Support Force (JSF) 78; Medical
  Laboratory (AML) 77; Nuclear
  Regulatory Commission 76; "War
  on Terror" 50
US-Japan Joint Declaration on
  Security 1996 49
US-Japan Mutual Security Treaty
  1960 71
US-Japan Security Treaty 1951
  2, 10, 22
US-Japan-South Korea Trilateral
  Coordination and Oversight
  Group (TCOG) 5

US Marine Corps 70, 77
USAF (United States Air Force) 77
USFJ (United States Forces,
  Japan) 25, 68–9, 71, 72,
  75–76, 77–80
USS Curtis Wilbur 73
USS Essex 76
USS Germantown 76
USS Harpers Ferry 76
USS McCampbell 73
USS Ronald Reagan 74, 76
USS Tortuga 78, 79
"utilitarian" mode 5

Vietnam War 30

Walsh, Patrick 74, 78
Waltz, Kenneth N. 4, 13n2, 30
Washington Post (newspaper) 42
Watanabe, Michio 37
Weber, Steve 13n4
Wendt, Alexander 6, 30
Western-centrism 31
Whiting, Allen S. 70
Wilcox, Paul 73
Willard, Robert 73, 75, 76
Wohlforth, William Curti 4
World War II 2

Yamagata Airport 78
Yamaguchi, Jirō 30
Yanai, Shunji 53
Yasuhiro, Nakasone 47n11
Yemen 35
Yomiuri Shimbun Seijibu (newspaper)
  51, 52–3, 60
Yoshida, Shigeru 20–1

Zakaria, Fareed 3–4
zoku giin bureaucrats 67n4
Zupančic, Rok 48n12